Sneakiest Uses
for Everyday Things

Sneakiest Uses
for Everyday Things

How to Make a Boomerang with a
Business Card, Convert a Pencil into
a Microphone, Make Animated Origami,
Turn a TV Tray into a Giant Robot, and
Create Alternative Energy Science Projects

Cy Tymony

**Andrews McMeel
Publishing,LLC**
Kansas City

08 09 10 TEN 5
ISBN-13: 978-0-7407-6874-3
ISBN-10: 0-7407-6874-3

Library of Congress Control Number: 2007922151

www.andrewsmcmeel.com

www.sneakyuses.com

Attention: Schools and Businesses

Andrews McMeel books are available at quantity discounts with bulk purchase for educational, business, or sales promotional use. For information, please write to: Special Sales Department, Andrews McMeel Publishing, LLC, 1130 Walnut Street, Kansas City, Missouri 64106.

Disclaimer

This book is for the entertainment and edification of its readers. While reasonable care has been exercised with respect to its accuracy, the publisher and the author assume no responsibility for errors or omissions in its content. Nor do we assume liability for any damages resulting from use of the information presented here.

This book contains references to electrical safety that *must* be observed. *Do not use AC power for any projects listed*. Do not place or store magnets near such magnetically sensitive media as videotapes, audiotapes, or computer disks.

Disparities in materials and design methods and the application of the components may cause your results to vary from those shown here. The publisher and the author disclaim any liability for injury that may result from the use, proper or improper, of the information contained in this book. We do not guarantee that the information contained herein is complete, safe, or accurate, nor should it be considered a substitute for your good judgment and common sense.

Nothing in this book should be construed or interpreted to infringe on the rights of other persons or to violate criminal statues. We urge you to obey all laws and respect all rights, including property rights, of others.

Contents

PART I
Sneaky Science Tricks . . . 1

PART II
Sneaky Gadgets . . . 45

PART III
Sneaky Energy Projects and Simulations . . . 91

Part IV
Bonus Sections . . . 139

Science and Technology Resources . . . 161

Foreword

I was one of those kids who loved to tear things apart and put them back together. Old black-and-white TVs, washing machine motors, and solenoids littered my basement. Countless hours would be spent dissecting and building electronic gadgets in the coolness of that dark refuge.

I was what we would call today a "geek." I even wore a pocket protector (and when I studied engineering in college, I collected four slide rules).

Those postwar days, in the late 1950s and '60s, were ripe for we subterranean gadgeteers. Lower Manhattan was filled with surplus electronic parts and WWII junk just waiting for vultures like myself to descend and buy them by the pound or part. Decades before the World Trade Center was ever built, the streets that define that neighborhood were cluttered with cardboard boxes and tables overflowing with resistors, vacuum tubes, circuit boards, and knobs of every kind. Radios and TVs spilled into the streets, and lucky was the kid who could afford to bring home the innards of a real, live radarscope. Who knows what ship it had served, what foreign planes had blipped across its screen? These were our fields of dreams, where hobbyists could find all the ingredients they needed for home-brew creations.

It was a paradise. And then I grew up. I left home, abandoning my Heathkits and *Popular Electronics* projects (I made a four-transistor radio!). My science fair punch-card reader collected dust, my oscilloscope never to be turned on again.

Those days of wonderful creativity slowly faded away, becoming cherished memories of youth. Modern computer chips made once-simple soldering techniques more risky and unnecessary. Heathkit went out of business. Radio Shack cut way back on its hobbyist section. The Internet captured most of my attention. My tinkering juices were never to be stirred up again, I thought.

Then I discovered Cy Tymony. His books drew me like a moth to a flame. There, amid the pages of hand-drawn illustrations, were the kinds of projects I hadn't seen in years. Decades. Half a lifetime. With a few twists of a screwdriver, you could turn an ordinary radio into a magical box where airline pilots talk to one other. You could make all kinds of "stuff" out all parts just lying around the house. I could tinker again!

Thank you, Cy, for reinvigorating those creative juices. We all owe you debt of gratitude for reinventing the old days for we veterans of the vacuum tube era. And for opening up the world of tinkering and creativity to a whole new generation of hobbyists looking to get their hands dirty with new and exciting projects.

Ira Flatow
Science Friday

Acknowledgments

Special thanks to my agents, Sheree Bykofsky and Janet Rosen, for believing in the book series from the start. I want to also thank Katie Anderson, my editor at Andrews McMeel, for her invaluable insights.

I'm also grateful to the following people who helped spread the word about the first two Sneaky Uses books:

Gayle Anderson, Ira Flatow, Susan Casey, Sandy Cohen, Katey Schwartz, Cherie Courtage, Mike Suan, John Schatzel, Mark Frauenfelder, Melissa Gwynne, Steve Cochran, Christopher G. Selfridge, Timothy M. Blangger, Charles Bergquist, Phillip M. Torrone, M. K. Donaldson, Paul MacGregor, David Chang, Jessica Warren, Steve Metsch, Jenifer N. Johnson, Jerry Davich, Jerry Reno, Austin Michael, Tony Lossano, Diane Lewis, Bob Kostanczuk, Marty Griffin, Mackenzie Miller, Rebecca Schuler, Larry Elder, Dennis Prager, Carlos Daza, Paul Scott, Ronald Mitchell, and Bruce Pasarow.

I'm thankful for the project evaluation and testing assistance provided by Bill Melzer, Sybil Smith, Isaac English, and Jerry Anderson.

And a special thanks to Clyde Tymony, Helen Cooper, and my mother, Cloise Shaw, for giving me positive inspiration, a foundation in science, and a love of reading.

Introduction

"Life is what you make it."

People rarely think about the common items and devices they use in everyday life. They think even less about adapting them to perform other functions.

You can easily learn how to become a real-life MacGyver using nothing but everyday items at your disposal. It doesn't hurt to have the smarts of Einstein or the strength of Superman, but they're not necessary with *Sneakiest Uses for Everyday Things*. When life puts you in a bind, the best solution is frequently not the obvious one. It'll be the sneaky one.

Solutions to a dilemma can come from the most unlikely sources:

- U.S. prisoners of war devised stealthy makeshift radio receivers using nothing more than a razor blade, a pencil, and wire from the wire fence from the prison camp as an antenna.
- Convicts at correctional institutions have used dental floss to saw through cell bars, and floss to braid a 20-foot rope to scale a wall. An inventive inmate escaped by using a Monopoly game piece, the wheelbarrow, to unscrew his ceiling vent. Another prisoner used a green felt-tipped pen to color a spare uniform green, and he walked out with the medical staff the next day.
- Prisoners of war at Germany's Colditz Castle prison during World War II used cotton sleeping bags, nails, and wood from floorboards in their cells to construct a two-man, 19-foot glider with a 33-foot wingspan. The resourceful prisoners made drills from the nails, saw handles from bed

boards, and saw blades from a wind-up record player's spring and from the frame around iron window bars. To cover the glider's wooden frame, they used bedsheets that they painted with hot millet (part of their rations) to stiffen the fabric. The flight never took place because the prisoners were rescued by the Americans in 1945. (Pictures and more details about the Colditz glider can be seen at www. sneakyuses.com.)

- On September 11, 2001, a window washer trapped in a Twin Towers elevator with five other passengers used his squeegee to pry open the doors and also to chisel through five layers of drywall material, to escape the inferno.

Thousands of you have bought the first two books in the series, *Sneaky Uses for Everyday Things* and *Sneakier Uses for Everyday Things,* and I am immensely grateful. I've asked for feedback and listened to your requests. Some parents wanted more nontechnical, easy-to-make projects using just paper and cardboard, which they could construct with their children. Others requested updates to projects in the first two books. In addition, the desire for more science projects was made clear.

I've kept your requests in mind while writing *Sneakiest Uses for Everyday Things.* It not only has a new assortment of sneaky gadget projects but includes 30 percent more material, including the aforementioned additions. Plus, a bonus "Science and Technology Resources" section provides the information you need to further explore science experimentation and education. You'll find links to city, state, and national science fairs, camps, schools, organizations, scholarships, inventor resources and contests, grants and awards, free government programs, educator lesson plans, and science projects Web sites.

Did you know that you can turn a screw into a motor? Or a bookmark into a boomerang? Want to know what common kitchen items can be turned into a modular 6-foot robot? It's in here. Want to know how oil is refined? Or how fuel cells work or nuclear energy is produced? That's here, too. *Sneakiest Uses for Everyday Things* avoids projects or procedures that require special or expensive materials not found in the average home. No special knowledge or tools are needed.

For lovers of self-reliance and gadgetry, *Sneakiest Uses for Everyday Things* is an amazing assortment of more than fifty-five fabulous science tricks, build-it yourself projects, alternative energy experiments and simulations, updates to projects from the previous *Sneaky Uses* books, and more.

Sneakiest Uses for Everyday Things can be used in many ways. Perhaps you like to conserve resources, or the idea of getting something for nothing. You can use the book as a practical tool, a fantasy escape, or a trivia guide; it's up to you. "Things" will never appear the same again. Let's start now.

You can do more than you think!

PART I

Sneaky Science Tricks

Science is sometimes difficult to understand but you can demonstrate its principles with household items you use every day. Using nothing but paper, cardboard from product packaging, paper clips, aluminum foil, paper cups, and refrigerator magnets, you can quickly perform sneaky science tricks.

In this part of *Sneakiest Uses for Everyday Things,* you'll learn sneaky sources for wire and how to connect things. You'll be shown how to make clever center-of-gravity balancing designs, a handheld Sneaky Boomerang, and a palm-size Sneaky Mini-Boomerang.

You'll also learn how to make additional Sneaky Flyers, including a paper plate flyer, a Styrofoam glider, and a hoop ring/straw flyer; an intercom with just speakers and no power source; a pencil that acts as a microphone, a tornado in a bottle, and more.

If you have an insatiable curiosity for sneaky secrets of everyday things, look no further. You can begin demonstrating clever resourcefulness right here.

Sneaky Wire Sources

Ordinary wire can be used in many sneaky ways. You'll soon learn how it can be utilized to make a radio transmitter, a speaker, and more.

When wire is required for sneaky projects, whenever possible try to use everyday items that you might otherwise have thrown away. Recycling metal will help save our natural resources.

Getting Wired

In an emergency, you can obtain wire—or items that can be used as wire—from some very unlikely sources. **Figure 1** illustrates just a few of the possible items that you can use in case connecting wire is not available.

Ready-to-use wire can be obtained from:
> Telephone cords
> TV/VCR cables
> Headphone wire
> Earphone wire
> Speaker wire
> Wire from inside toys, radios,
> and other electrical devices

Note: Some of the sources above will have one to six separate wires inside.

Wire for projects can also be made from:
>   Take-out food container handles
>   Twist-ties
>   Paper clips
>   Envelope clasps
>   Ballpoint pen springs
>   Fast-food wrappers
>   Potato chip bag liners

You can also use aluminum from the following items:
>   Margarine wrappers
>   Ketchup and condiment packages
>   Breath mint container labels
>   Chewing gum wrappers
>   Trading card packaging
>   Coffee creamer container lids

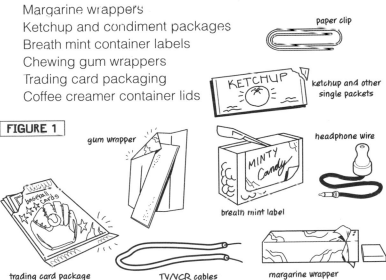

FIGURE 1

paper clip

ketchup and other single packets

gum wrapper

headphone wire

MINTY Candy

breath mint label

trading card package

TV/VCR cables

margarine wrapper

Note: The wire used from the sources above are only to be used for low-voltage, battery-powered projects.

Use special care when handling fragile aluminum materials. In some instances, aluminum may be coated with a wax or plastic coating that you may be able to remove.

You can cut strips of aluminum material from food wrappers easily enough. With smaller items—such as aluminum obtained from a coffee cream container—use the sneaky cutting pattern shown in **Figure 2**.

Making resourceful use of items to make sneaky wire is not only intriguing, it's fun.

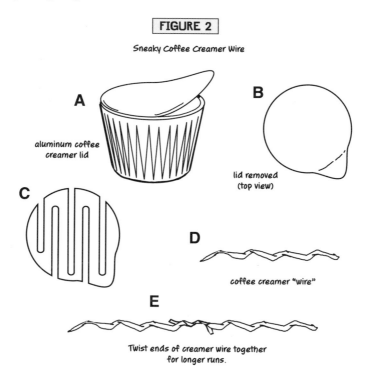

FIGURE 2

Sneaky Coffee Creamer Wire

A

aluminum coffee creamer lid

B

lid removed (top view)

C

D

coffee creamer "wire"

E

Twist ends of creamer wire together for longer runs.

How to Connect Things

The "Getting Wired" project illustrated how to obtain wire from everyday things. Now you'll learn how to connect the wires to provide consistent performance. (A tight connection is crucial to the operation of electrical projects, otherwise faulty and erratic result may occur.)

Figure 1 shows a piece of insulated wire. The insulation material must be stripped away to make a metal-to-metal connection to other electrical parts. Strip away about one to two inches of insulation from both ends of the wire. See **Figure 2**.

To connect the wire to another wire lead, wrap both ends around each other, as shown in **Figure 3**.

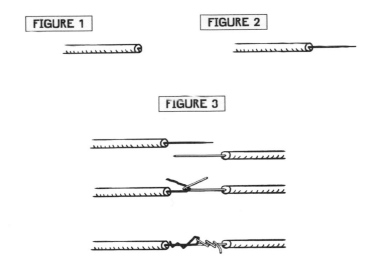

When connecting the wire to the end of a stiff lead (such as the end of an LED), wrap the wire around the lead and bend the lead back over the wire. See **Figure 4**.

To connect wire to the end of a small battery, bend the wire into a circular shape, place it on the battery terminal, and wrap the connection tightly with tape, as shown in **Figure 5**.

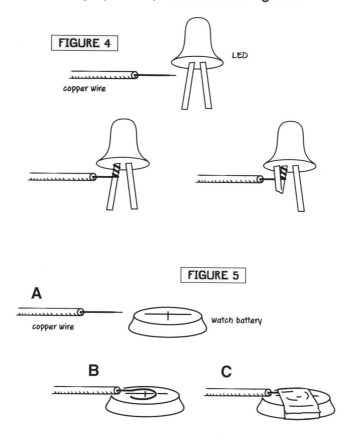

Electricity Fun-damentals

Many forms of alternative energy, including wind, thermal, hydro, even nuclear, are used to generate electrical power. This is accomplished by moving blades (wind or hydro) or heating water into steam (thermal or nuclear) to turn an electrical generator. The following projects illustrate how electrical power is produced and the relationship between electricity and magnetism.

What's Needed

Transparent tape
Two D-size batteries
Wire
Compass
Two small, strong magnets
Bolt
Paper clips

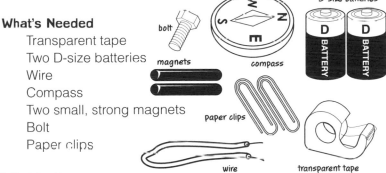

What to Do

When electricity flows through a wire, a magnetic field is produced around it. To test this, first tape the two D-size batteries together and place them near a length of wire. Next, set the compass near the wire and hold the ends of the wire to both battery terminals (only for a few seconds), and you'll see the compass pointer move. See **Figure 1**.

Position the wire vertically in a small loop shape and touch the battery terminals. Bring a magnet close to the wire as you connect and disconnect the wire, and you'll see the wire move because it has become an electromagnet. See **Figure 2**.

If you wrap wire thirty times around a bolt and connect it to the battery terminals, it will become an electromagnet. **Figure 3** shows how it can attract and lift paper clips.

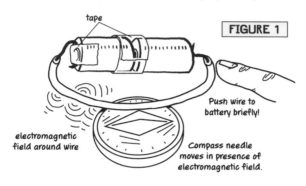

tape

FIGURE 1

Push wire to battery briefly!

electromagnetic field around wire

Compass needle moves in presence of electromagnetic field.

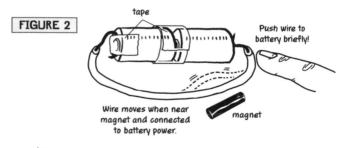

tape

FIGURE 2

Push wire to battery briefly!

Wire moves when near magnet and connected to battery power.

magnet

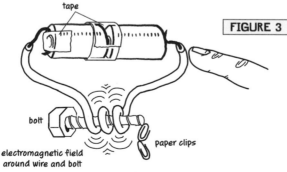

tape

FIGURE 3

bolt

paper clips

electromagnetic field around wire and bolt

Simple Electrical Circuits

To test an item's conductivity (the ability to let electricity to flow through it), use a flashlight bulb or an LED (light emitting diode). An LED is used in most electronic devices and toys as a function indicator because it draws very little electrical current, operates with very little heat, and has no filament to burn out.

Lay a 3-volt watch battery on the item, as shown in **Figure 1**. If the lightbulb or LED lights, then the item can be used as wire for battery powered projects.

Note: If the bulb or LED does not light, reverse the connections of its leads and test it again. LEDs are polarity (direction) sensitive.

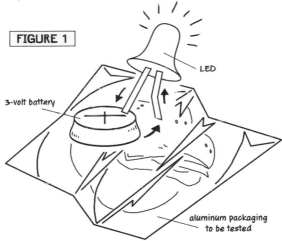

FIGURE 1

LED

3-volt battery

aluminum packaging to be tested

Current flows from the battery's negative (-) terminal to the aluminum foil to the LED to the battery's positive (+) terminal in a circle.

Figure 2 shows a simple electrical circuit that consists of a battery, connecting wire, and a lightbulb. Power flows in a circle (*circuit* means "circle") from the negative battery terminal to the light and back to the positive battery terminal.

When using one 1½-volt battery in a circuit, you must use a lightbulb rated the same voltage. This applies to whatever else you may want to turn on, such as a buzzer or motor.

LEDs generally require two to three volts (unless otherwise noted) to turn on, so connect two 1½-volt batteries in series (end to end) to activate an LED.

Figure 3 illustrates how to do this. If the LED does not turn on, reverse its leads and test it again.

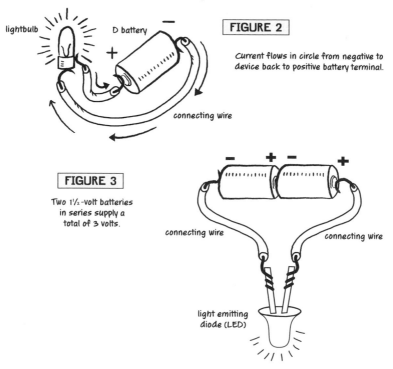

lightbulb   D battery   **−**   **FIGURE 2**

Current flows in circle from negative to device back to positive battery terminal.

connecting wire

FIGURE 3

Two 1½-volt batteries in series supply a total of 3 volts.

connecting wire   connecting wire

light emitting diode (LED)

Sneaky Balance Tricks

You can make everyday things balance in sneaky ways when you know the secret to determining the center of gravity. The center of gravity is the point in an object at which its mass is in equilibrium. Where this point is depends on the object's shape and weight distribution, and you can produce some attention-getting creations with this knowledge.

The following four projects are easy to do with items found just about everywhere.

Sneaky Balancer I

Knowing how to lower the center of gravity of an object allows you to produce figures that seemingly defy gravity (or make you seem like a skilled magician). This project demonstrates what happens when two similar cardboard figures have their center of gravity in different positions.

What's Needed

Scissors
Cardboard, a piece 8½ by 11 inches
Optional:
Sewing thread

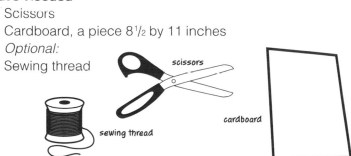

What to Do

Cut out the small shape shown in **Figure 1** from the piece of
cardboard. Follow the dimensions shown. Next, try to balance
the head of the figure on your fingertip, as shown in **Figure 2**.
It's almost impossible to keep it upright without its tipping over.

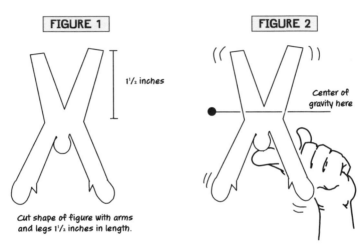

FIGURE 1

1¹/₂ inches

Cut shape of figure with arms
and legs 1¹/₂ inches in length.

FIGURE 2

Center of
gravity here

Try to balance the figure's head on
your finger, and the figure falls.

Next, cut out the figure shown in **Figure 3**. The only
difference is the legs are much longer. Try to balance this larger
figure on your hand. It's easy now, because the center of gravity
is below your finger. See **Figure 4**. You should be able to walk
around the room and the figure will not fall.

Going Further

To demonstrate how acrobats keep their balance, cut a small slit
in the head of the figure. See **Figure 5**.

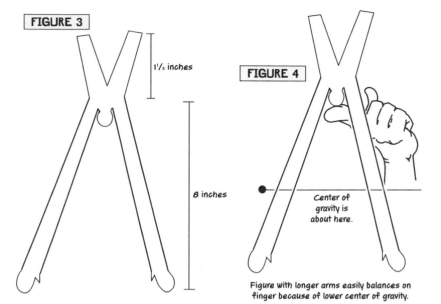

FIGURE 3

1¹/₂ inches

8 inches

FIGURE 4

Center of
gravity is
about here.

Figure with longer arms easily balances on
finger because of lower center of gravity.

Then, tie a length of thread from a chair to a lower object, such as another chair or table, and set the figure on the thread. The figure should rest on the thread in its slit and, with a slight push, slide across without falling. See **Figure 6**.

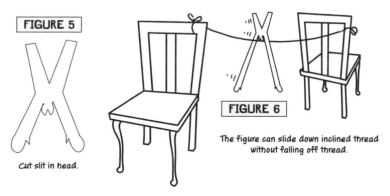

FIGURE 5

Cut slit in head.

FIGURE 6

The figure can slide down inclined thread
without falling off thread.

Sneaky Balancer II

This sneaky balancer can rest horizontally on the tip of a paper clip and will surely astonish onlookers.

What's Needed
Scissors
Cardboard
Paper clip

What to Do
Cut out the figure shown in **Figure 1** from the piece of cardboard. Be sure to include the spiked hair, with a long center spike. Try to adhere to the dimensions shown but, if desired, you can produce a larger or smaller figure as long as you keep the arm and body lengths in proportion.

Bend the figure's arms down at the shoulder and elbows. See **Figure 2**.

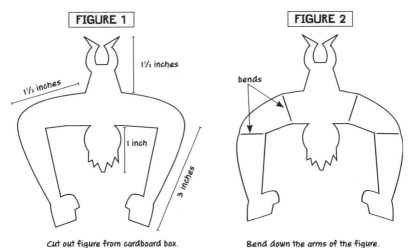

Cut out figure from cardboard box.

Bend down the arms of the figure.

Next, bend a paper clip, as shown in **Figure 3**, so one end stands up vertically.

Last, place the figure on the paper clip with the spiked hair resting on the tip. If necessary, bend the arms down so it won't fall. The figure should balance on the tip of the paper clip. You should be able to carefully push its legs to the right or left and it will stay aloft. See **Figure 4**.

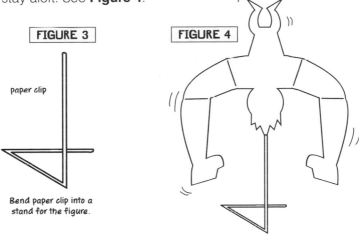

| FIGURE 3 |

paper clip

Bend paper clip into a stand for the figure.

| FIGURE 4 |

Gently rest head of figure on tip of paper clip and it will magically balance.

Sneaky Balancer III

What's Needed
Scissors
Cardboard, 8½ by 11 inches

scissors

cardboard

What to Do

Cut out the shape shown in **Figure 1** from the cardboard. Be careful to follow the dimensions shown.

You should be able to easily balance the figure on the tip of your finger, elbow, or nose, because its center of gravity is at the large circular area. See **Figure 2**.

You can create similar figures and, using paper clips or coins secured with tape, add weight to an area near the bottom section of the figure so it balances effortlessly.

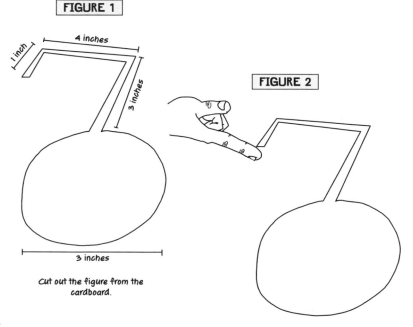

FIGURE 1

4 inches

1 inch

3 inches

3 inches

Cut out the figure from the cardboard.

FIGURE 2

Since the center of gravity is low, the figure will balance easily.

Sneaky Balancer IV

What's Needed
One quarter
Two metal forks
Drinking cup

What to Do
Place the quarter between the teeth of the two forks as shown in
Figure 1.

If a lightweight cup is used, you must fill it with water so
it will not tip over. If a heavy cup or jar is used, water is not
required.

Carefully rest the edge of the quarter on the lip of the cup.
You should be able to let go and the forks will stay aloft. If
they don't, adjust the angle of the forks until they balance. See
Figure 2.

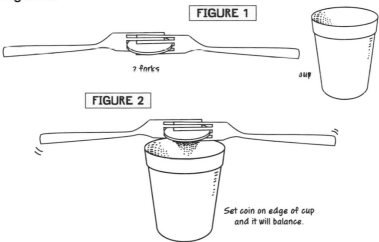

FIGURE 1

2 forks

cup

FIGURE 2

Set coin on edge of cup
and it will balance.

Sneaky Flyers

Sneaky Demonstrations of Air Pressure and Wing Lift

Have you ever wondered how airplanes and helicopters are able to fly? If you have, and want to demonstrate this principle, all you need are such ordinary items as straws, postcards, and strips of paper.

Air Pressure Demonstration I

An ordinary straw can be used to demonstrate that air pressure is all around us (15 pounds per square inch, to be exact). You can demonstrate this easily enough with everyday items.

What's Needed
> Straw
> Glass filled with water

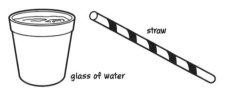

What to Do

Insert a straw into the glass of water, as shown in **Figure 1**. Next, place a finger over the top of the straw and lift it out of the water. See **Figure 2**.

You'll see that the water stays in the straw and doesn't flow out because air pressure from the bottom is keeping it in, as shown in **Figure 3**. When you lift your finger from the top of the straw, air pressure flows from the top and pushes against the water, forcing it out.

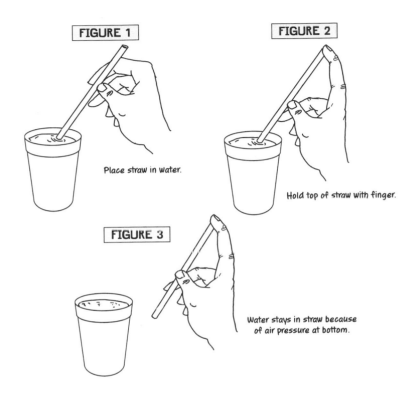

FIGURE 1

Place straw in water.

FIGURE 2

Hold top of straw with finger.

FIGURE 3

Water stays in straw because of air pressure at bottom.

Air Pressure Demonstration II

You can demonstrate the power of air pressure in a more dramatic way with the following project, again using everyday items.

What's Needed
Glass filled to the brim with water
Plastic-coated postcard

postcard

glass of water

What to Do

Working over a sink, hold up the glass of water. Place a postcard over the mouth of the glass and turn the glass upside down, holding the postcard in place with your finger under it, as shown in **Figure 1**.

Carefully remove your finger from the postcard and you should see that the postcard will not fall. With no air in the glass to push against the postcard, the air outside presses against the postcard, keeping it in place, even with the weight of the water upon it. See **Figure 2**.

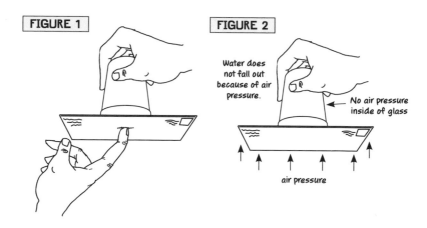

FIGURE 1

FIGURE 2

Water does not fall out because of air pressure.

No air pressure inside of glass

air pressure

Air Pressure Demonstration III

What's Needed

Paper (preferably a paper towel or napkin)
Scissors

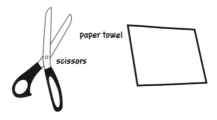

paper towel

scissors

What to Do

Cut a paper strip ½ inch wide by 4 inches in length as shown in **Figure 1**. Hold the paper strip up to your face above your mouth and blow. The paper naturally moves upward. Now hold the paper strip just below your lips and blow above the strip. As shown in **Figure 2**, the paper will also rise and move upward!

This occurs because of Bernoulli's principle, which states that fast-moving air has less pressure than nonmoving air. The air under the strip has more pressure than the air above it and pushes the strip upward.

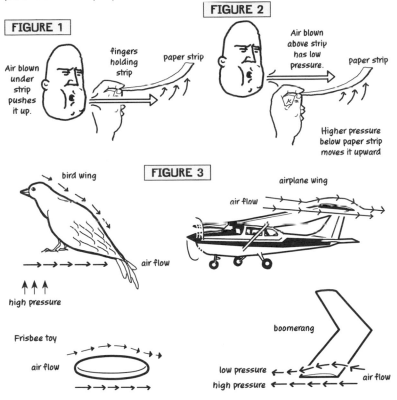

Figure 3 illustrates a side view of a bird's wing, an airplane wing, a Frisbee flying disk, and a boomerang. Notice the top of the wing curves upward and has a longer surface as compared to the bottom. When the airplane moves forward, air moves above and below the wing. The air moving along the curved top must travel farther and faster than the air moving past the flat bottom surface. The faster-moving air has less pressure than the air at the bottom and this provides lift.

Baseball pitchers can take advantage of Bernoulli's principle by releasing the ball with a forward spin. The ball produces a lower pressure below it, causing it to dip when it reaches the plate. Hence, a curveball. See **Figure 4**.

Sailboats apply Bernoulli's principle to use the wind, regardless of its direction, to propel the boat in any desired direction. **Figure 5** shows how altering the shape of the sail into a curve produces an effect similar to that of an airplane wing. The wind moves at a faster rate over the curved side, with a lower pressure, and the higher pressure on the other side of the sail pushes the boat laterally. A centerboard, attached to the boat hull, prevents the boat from moving sideways while allowing it to use the wind thrust to move forward. See **Figure 6**.

Automobile bodies are similar to an airplane wing because they are flat on the bottom and curved on top. They can lose stability at high speeds since they tend to achieve lift from the higher air pressure below, as shown in **Figure 7**. To reduce the Bernoulli effect, automakers have incorporated improvements in vehicle design, such as lowering the body height, adding special front bumper and fender contours, and installing rear spoilers. See **Figure 8**.

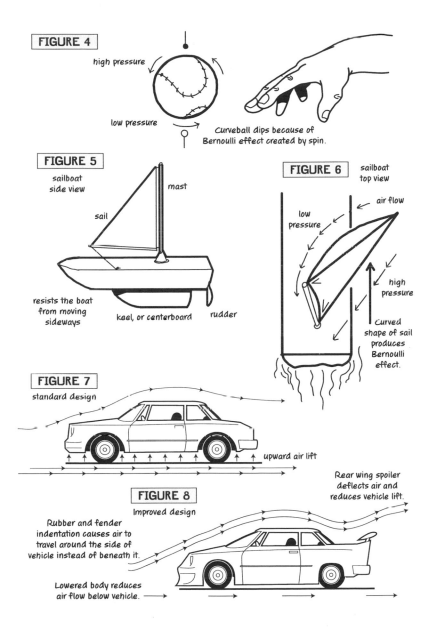

FIGURE 4

high pressure

low pressure

Curveball dips because of Bernoulli effect created by spin.

FIGURE 5

sailboat side view

mast

sail

resists the boat from moving sideways

keel, or centerboard

rudder

FIGURE 6

sailboat top view

air flow

low pressure

high pressure

Curved shape of sail produces Bernoulli effect.

FIGURE 7

standard design

upward air lift

FIGURE 8

Improved design

Rear wing spoiler deflects air and reduces vehicle lift.

Rubber and fender indentation causes air to travel around the side of vehicle instead of beneath it.

Lowered body reduces air flow below vehicle.

Air Pressure Demonstration IV

What's Needed

Scissors

Paper (preferably a paper towel or napkin)

Two empty soda cans

Magazine

scissors

paper towel

soda cans

magazine

What to Do

Cut two paper strips ¹/₂ inch wide by 4 inches in length and hold them about 2 inches apart, as shown in **Figure 1**. Blow air between the paper strips and watch what occurs. You would expect the strips to blow apart but they actually come together, as shown in **Figure 2**.

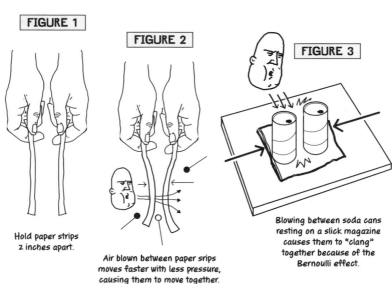

FIGURE 1

Hold paper strips 2 inches apart.

FIGURE 2

Air blown between paper srips moves faster with less pressure, causing them to move together.

FIGURE 3

Blowing between soda cans resting on a slick magazine causes them to "clang" together because of the Bernoulli effect.

Bernoulli's principle is working here because the faster-moving air blown between the paper strips has less pressure than the air on the other side of the paper. This higher pressure pushes the strips toward each other.

Now, place the two empty soda cans an inch apart upon the slick surface of a magazine. When you blow between the cans, they will move toward each other, producing a clanging sound. See **Figure 3**.

Air Pressure Demonstration V

Here's another sneaky, easy-to-perform demonstration of air pressure's causing an unexpected result.

What's Needed
   Scissors
   Piece of paper

What to Do
Cut the piece of paper into a 5 by 3-inch shape. Fold the paper in half lengthwise, as shown in **Figure 1**.

Next, unfold the paper and place it on a flat surface so that it has a slight rise near its center crease. See **Figure 2**.

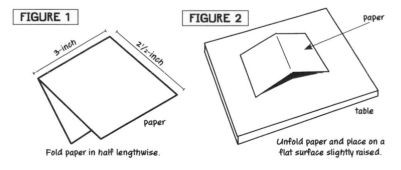

| FIGURE 1 |
Fold paper in half lengthwise.

| FIGURE 2 |
Unfold paper and place on a flat surface slightly raised.

Then, as shown in **Figure 3**, bring your face close to the surface of the table and blow underneath the paper.

You would expect the paper to rise but it actually flattens downward. The higher air pressure on top of the paper, compared to the fast-moving air beneath it, pushes the paper flat on the table, as shown in **Figure 4**.

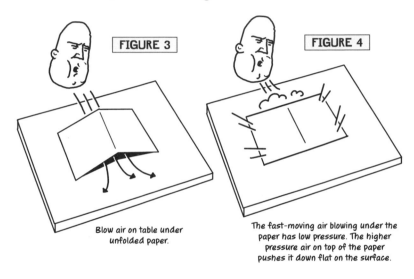

| FIGURE 3 | FIGURE 4 |

Blow air on table under unfolded paper.

The fast-moving air blowing under the paper has low pressure. The higher pressure air on top of the paper pushes it down flat on the surface.

Air Pressure Demonstration VI

You can use Bernoulli's principle to perform a neat magic trick by making a ball rise from a cup and jump into another one without touching it.

Ping-Pong ball

small cups

What's Needed
    Ping-Pong ball
    Two small cups

What to Do

This project requires small cups that are slightly smaller in diameter than the Ping-Pong ball. Since the Ping-Pong ball can barely fit in the cup, rapidly moving air above the ball will not affect the air pressure beneath it.

Put the ball into one of the cups and place it about 3 inches away from the second cup, as shown in **Figure 1**. Blow as hard as you can above the first cup and the ball should start to rise. See **Figure 2**. The force of your breath will push the raised Ping-Pong ball over to the empty cup, where it will drop inside, as shown in **Figure 3**. With a little practice, you can make this sneaky trick work every time.

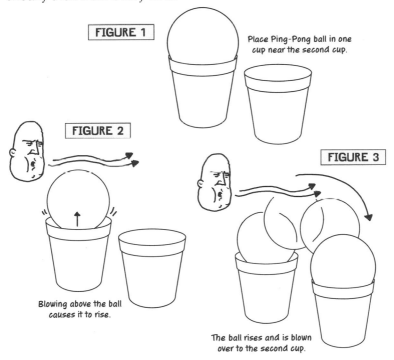

FIGURE 1

Place Ping-Pong ball in one cup near the second cup.

FIGURE 2

Blowing above the ball causes it to rise.

FIGURE 3

The ball rises and is blown over to the second cup.

Sneaky Flying Disk

You've seen how Bernoulli's principle works. Now it's time to put it to use and make a sneaky flyer, similar to flying disk toys, using paper and tape.

What's Needed
Scissors
Paper, 8½ x 11 inches
Transparent tape

What to Do
Cut eight 2-inch square pieces of paper as shown in **Figure 1**. Fold the top right corner of one square down to the lower left corner. See **Figure 2**. Then, fold the top left corner down to the bottom, as shown in **Figure 3**.

Repeat these two folds with the remaining seven squares. See **Figure 4**.

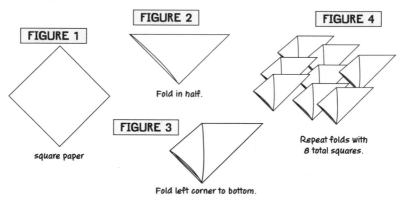

FIGURE 1
square paper

FIGURE 2
Fold in half.

FIGURE 3
Fold left corner to bottom.

FIGURE 4
Repeat folds with 8 total squares.

Insert one paper figure into the left pocket of another, as shown in **Figure 5**. Repeat inserting the figures into one another until they form an eight-sided doughnut shape; see **Figure 6**. Apply tape as needed to keep the origami flyer together and turn over, as shown in **Figure 7**.

Next, bend up the outer edge of the sneaky flyer to form a lip, as shown in **Figure 8**. This outer lip will cause the air to take a longer path over it, producing a Bernoulli effect.

Turn the device so the lip is bent downward. Throw the Sneaky Flying Disk with a quick snap of your wrist and it should stay aloft for a great distance.

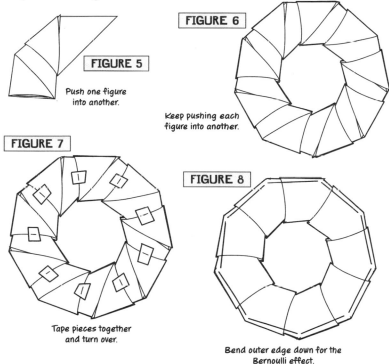

FIGURE 5

Push one figure into another.

FIGURE 6

Keep pushing each figure into another.

FIGURE 7

Tape pieces together and turn over.

FIGURE 8

Bend outer edge down for the Bernoulli effect.

Sneaky Boomerang

Want a sneaky way to play catch alone? You just need a piece of cardboard and foam rubber to make a working boomerang that will actually fly up to 30 feet away and return.

What's Needed

Scissors
Cardboard from a food box
Foam rubber, from an old pillow
Transparent tape

cardboard box

tape

foam rubber

scissors

What to Do

Cut the cardboard into the boomerang shape shown in **Figure 1**. Each wing of the boomerang should be 9 inches long by 2 inches wide.

Then, cut two foam pieces into 6 by 2-inch oval shapes with one side rising into a curve. The rising shape should resemble the side view of an airplane wing. See **Figure 2**. Place the oval foam pieces on the leading edges of the boomerang and secure them with tape.

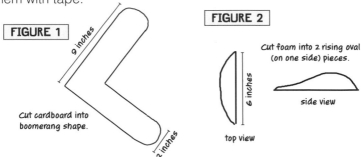

FIGURE 1

9 inches

2 inches

Cut cardboard into boomerang shape.

FIGURE 2

Cut foam into 2 rising oval (on one side) pieces.

6 inches

top view

side view

Note: Look carefully at the placement of the ovals on the boomerang wings in **Figure 3** before taping them. The foam creates a curved shape on the boomerang wing, which will cause air to move faster across its top than across the bottom surface. This will produce lift for the boomerang.

Hold the boomerang as if you were going to throw a baseball and throw it straight overhead (not to the side). See **Figure 4**. The Sneaky Boomerang should fly straight and return to the left. Experiment with different angles of throw to obtain a desired return pattern.

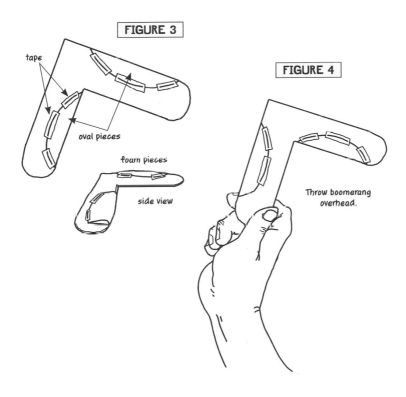

FIGURE 3

tape

oval pieces

foam pieces

side view

FIGURE 4

Throw boomerang overhead.

Sneaky Mini-Boomerang

You can use postcards, business cards, or cardboard food boxes to make a miniature, palm-size boomerang that actually flies and returns to you, for indoor fun.

What's Needed

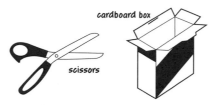

cardboard box

Scissors
Cardboard from food
    boxes or postcards

scissors

What to Do

Cut out the boomerang shapes shown in **Figure 1**. The boomerang wings can be any length between 2 to 4 inches. For optimal flight height and return performance, cut each wing of the boomerang 2$\frac{1}{2}$ inches long and $\frac{1}{2}$ inch wide.

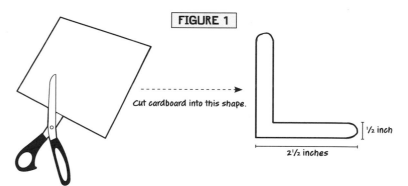

FIGURE 1

Cut cardboard into this shape.

$\frac{1}{2}$ inch

2$\frac{1}{2}$ inches

Set the Sneaky Mini-Boomerang on the palm of your raised hand with one wing hanging off. Tilt your hand slightly upward. With your other hand's thumb and middle finger $1/2$ inch away, snap the outer boomerang wing. You'll discover (after a few attempts) that it will fly forward and return to you. See **Figure 2**.

Note: You must snap your finger with a strong snapping action to make the boomerang fly away and return properly, as shown in **Figure 3**.

Experiment with different hand positions and angles to control the boomerang's flight pattern.

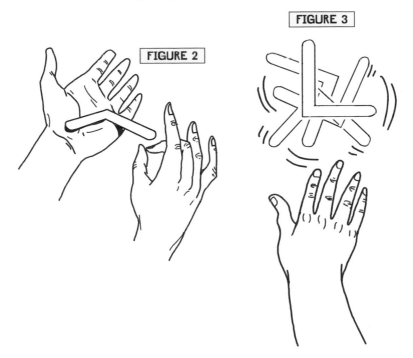

FIGURE 3

FIGURE 2

Sneaky Gliders

You don't have to spend money on a balsa wood kit to make a simple working glider. A working glider, made from discarded cardboard or Styrofoam material, can produce plenty of sneaky flyers for safe fun.

What's Needed

Scissors
Flat corrugated cardboard or Styrofoam
Transparent tape

What to Do

The sneaky glider body, or fuselage, can be cut out from the pattern shown in **Figure 1**. The plane will require at least one wing near the center for stability. A smaller wing near the rear rudder can also be added. Simply insert the wing(s) into the body slits and use tape to secure them properly as shown in **Figure 2**.

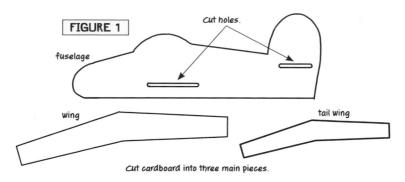

Cut cardboard into three main pieces.

Launch the Sneaky Glider with a snap of the wrist near your ear and it should fly up to 30 feet away. See **Figure 3**. Test the glider wing(s) shapes to achieve various flight paths as desired.

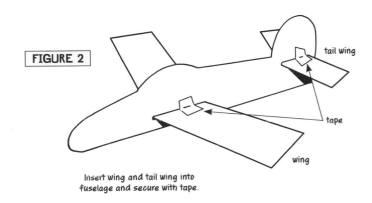

FIGURE 2

tail wing

tape

wing

Insert wing and tail wing into
fuselage and secure with tape.

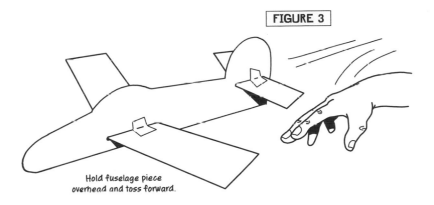

FIGURE 3

Hold fuselage piece
overhead and toss forward.

Sneaky Hoop Paper Flyer

Paper airplane designs are not hard to find. But if you want to stand out from the crowd, make this unique sneaky flyer using just a straw and paper.

What's Needed

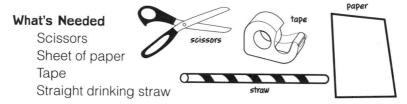

Scissors
Sheet of paper
Tape
Straight drinking straw

What to Do

First, cut two paper strips ½ inch wide by 4 inches long and then tape each strip into a loop, as shown in **Figure 1**. Next, tape a loop to each end of the straw. See **Figure 2**.

Now launch the sneaky straw flyer with your hand as if you were throwing a dart. It should fly up to 40 feet away.

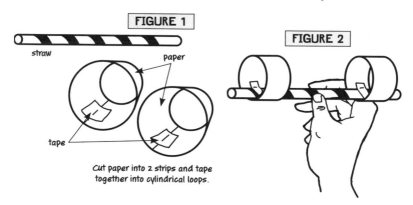

FIGURE 1

FIGURE 2

Cut paper into 2 strips and tape
together into cylindrical loops.

Sneaky Soaring Cylinder

Paper airplanes don't have to have a standard-looking shape to glide long distances. Believe it or not, you can fold an ordinary piece of paper into the shape of a cup and amaze your friends with a Sneaky Soaring Cylinder.

What's Needed
Sheet of paper

paper

What to Do

First, fold the left side of the paper 2 inches to the right, as shown in **Figure 1**. Next, fold the paper from the left side one more inch, and crease it firmly. See **Figure 2**.

Roll the paper into a cylinder, then slide one end of the paper into the other end's folded-over area, as shown in **Figure 3**. Push the left side of the paper into the right side until about two inches' worth is securely in place. Then, roll over and firmly crease the edge of the folded paper into a lip to secure it. See **Figures 4** and **5**.

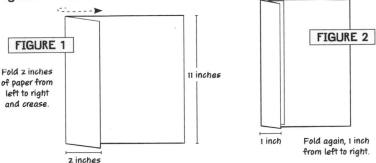

FIGURE 1

Fold 2 inches of paper from left to right and crease.

11 inches

2 inches

FIGURE 2

1 inch   Fold again, 1 inch from left to right.

Next, bend over the top layer of paper into a fin shape, shown in **Figure 6**, so it stands vertically. This will act as a wind stabilizer to keep the cylinder in the air.

Last, toss the cylinder like a football, but don't add a spinning motion. See **Figure 7**. The Sneaky Soaring Cylinder should fly up to 40 feet away. Experiment with the shape of the stabilizer fin to achieve the desired various flight paths.

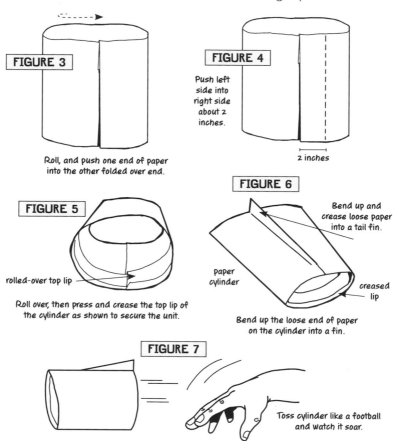

FIGURE 3

Roll, and push one end of paper into the other folded over end.

FIGURE 4

Push left side into right side about 2 inches.

2 inches

FIGURE 5

rolled-over top lip

Roll over, then press and crease the top lip of the cylinder as shown to secure the unit.

FIGURE 6

Bend up and crease loose paper into a tail fin.

paper cylinder

creased lip

Bend up the loose end of paper on the cylinder into a fin.

FIGURE 7

Toss cylinder like a football and watch it soar.

Sneaky Intercom

Like motors and generators, speakers are made with magnets and coils of wires. By connecting two of them together with connecting wire, you can create a sneaky intercom that requires no external power source. This project also demonstrates the versatility of coils of wire and magnets.

wire

speakers

What's Needed

2 speakers (not mounted in a case)
Fifty feet (or more) of wire,
cut into two wires

What to Do

As illustrated in **Figure 1**, connect both wires to each speaker and wrap them tightly around the lug connections. If you carefully press the cone of one speaker, the other should move.

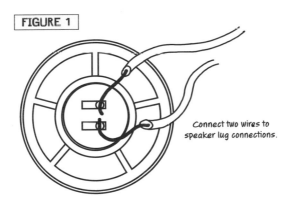

FIGURE 1

Connect two wires to speaker lug connections.

Pressing the speaker cone, with the speaker coil, or voice coil, of wire attached to it generates an electrical current as it moves near the speaker's internal magnet. This current travels through the wire and into the other speaker's coil, creating an electromagnetic field. This causes its voice coil to repel against the magnet and move rapidly, producing sound.

The field is repelled by the speaker's magnet and moves slightly. Now, with the speakers separated, talk loudly in one speaker and have a friend listen to the other, as shown in **Figure 2**.

Your voice will be heard. Congratulations, you've just completed a no-electrical-power-supplied Sneaky Intercom.

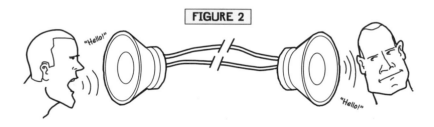

FIGURE 2

Sneaky Pencil Microphone

A typical pencil contains graphite (not actual lead) that can be used as a resistor. A resistor impedes the flow of electrical current and, if its value is varied, can carry sound in an electrical circuit.

A bare pencil lead placed on two others can act as a microphone.

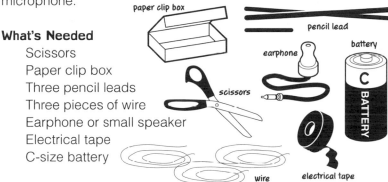

What's Needed

Scissors
Paper clip box
Three pencil leads
Three pieces of wire
Earphone or small speaker
Electrical tape
C-size battery

What to Do

Cut four holes in the box and slide two pencil leads into the holes, as shown in **Figure 1**. Next, lay the third lead rod, broken to be half the length of the others, on the other two, as shown in **Figure 2**.

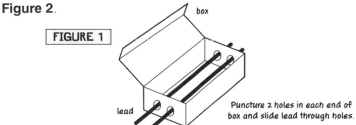

FIGURE 1

box

lead

Puncture 2 holes in each end of box and slide lead through holes.

Connect two of the wires to the earphone/speaker. Of those two, connect one to a pencil lead sticking out of the box and the other to the battery terminal, using tape to secure it. Then tape the third wire from the battery and connect it to the other pencil lead. See **Figure 3**.

Now bring your mouth close to the small rod of lead and speak loudly. The sound will be heard from the speaker. Your voice moves the pencil lead on the other two pieces and changes its resistance level, which modulates the current flow. The earphone reproduces this as sound waves.

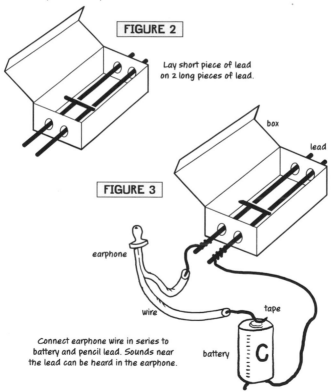

FIGURE 2

Lay short piece of lead on 2 long pieces of lead.

box

lead

FIGURE 3

earphone

wire

tape

battery

Connect earphone wire in series to battery and pencil lead. Sounds near the lead can be heard in the earphone.

Sneaky Tornado in a Bottle

You can produce a simulation of a tornado, using two-liter bottles and a few other common household items.

two-liter bottles

electrical tape

What's Needed
Two empty two-liter bottles,
    washed and dried
Scissors
Stiff, flat plastic from product
    packaging, or a 1-inch washer
Electrical tape

scissors   flat plastic

What to Do
Fill one bottle with water nearly all of the way to the top. See **Figure 1**.

Cut a 1-inch circle from the piece of stiff plastic, then cut a small hole in the center, $^3/_8$ inch in diameter, as shown in **Figure 2**, or use a 1-inch washer

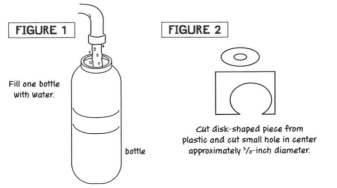

| FIGURE 1 | FIGURE 2 |

Fill one bottle
with water.

bottle

Cut disk-shaped piece from
plastic and cut small hole in center
approximately $^3/_8$-inch diameter.

Place the disk on top of the bottle filled with water, as shown in **Figure 3**, and place the other bottle on top of it (mouth to mouth), as shown in **Figure 4**. Wrap electrical tape tightly around the two bottle threads, as shown in **Figure 5**.

Turn the bottles upside down. As the water flows from the top to the bottom, air from the lower bottle will flow into the top, forming a swirling tornado-like vortex. See **Figure 6**. If this does not happen immediately or if the water just slowly drips down, shake the bottles to start the water flowing.

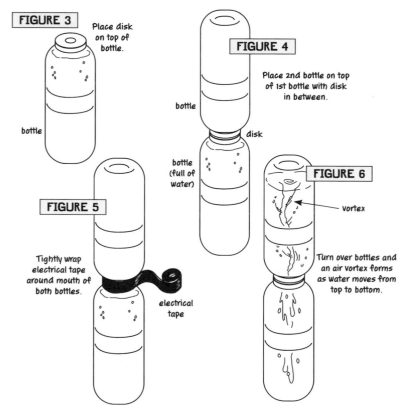

FIGURE 3

Place disk on top of bottle.

bottle

FIGURE 4

Place 2nd bottle on top of 1st bottle with disk in between.

bottle

disk

bottle (full of water)

FIGURE 5

Tightly wrap electrical tape around mouth of both bottles.

electrical tape

FIGURE 6

vortex

Turn over bottles and an air vortex forms as water moves from top to bottom.

PART II

Sneaky Gadgets

If you're curious about the sneaky adaptation possibilities of household devices, you're in the right place. People frequently throw away damaged gadgets and toys without realizing they can serve additional purposes.

This part of *Sneakiest Uses for Everyday Things* presents sneaky adaptation methods to make paper into animated origami designs, sugar into glass, a cup into a calculator, a quiz tester, motors, and robots, including a version that's six feet tall.

All the items have tested safe and can be made in no time. If you enjoy the idea of high-tech resourcefulness, the following projects will undoubtedly provide plenty of resourceful ideas.

You, too, can do more with less!

Sneaky Animated Origami

Paper folding is fun but you can enhance your enjoyment by making the following sneaky origami designs that include motion action using everyday things.

Sneaky Head-Bobbing Bird

What's Needed
  Scissors
  Paper
  Pencil

What to Do
Cut the paper into a square and fold/unfold both the diagonals, as shown in **Figure 1**. Fold over the top left and right corners to the center. See **Figure 2**.

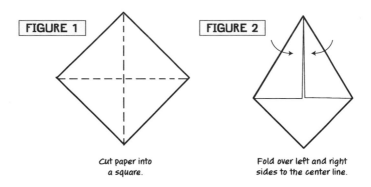

FIGURE 1

Cut paper into
a square.

FIGURE 2

Fold over left and right
sides to the center line.

Then, fold over the lower left and right corners toward the center as shown in **Figure 3**. Fold up the bottom point to the center line to form a tail and fold the top corner toward the back of the figure to make the head, as shown in **Figures 4** and **5**.

Next, fold the figure in half vertically along the center toward the tail. This will bend the tail and head outward as shown in **Figure 6**. Draw eyes and a beak on the figure as desired.

Last, with the sneaky bird standing upright, push down on the center of the tail. The head should move downward. See **Figure 7**.

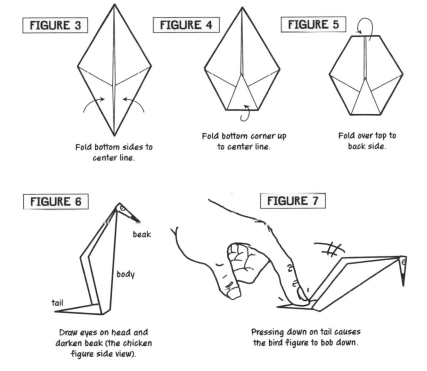

FIGURE 3	FIGURE 4	FIGURE 5
Fold bottom sides to center line.	Fold bottom corner up to center line.	Fold over top to back side.

FIGURE 6

beak

body

tail

Draw eyes on head and darken beak (the chicken figure side view).

FIGURE 7

Pressing down on tail causes the bird figure to bob down.

Sneaky Mouth Flapper

What's Needed

Scissors
Paper
Pencil

What to Do

Cut the paper into a square, as shown in **Figure 1**. Next, fold and unfold the square on both the diagonals. Fold over the lower left and right corners to the center. See **Figure 2**.

Then, fold over the upper left and right corners toward the center, as shown in **Figure 3**. Fold up the bottom half of the figure along the center crease. See **Figure 4**. Fold down the top front corner to the bottom of the figure, as shown in **Figure 5**.

Fold the top back tip down and to the left along the fold line shown in **Figure 5**. Then, fold the bottom front tip up and to the left along its indicated diagonal fold line, until it resembles the shape in **Figure 6**. Unfold the left-pointing tips back to their positions shown in **Figure 5**. See **Figure 7**.

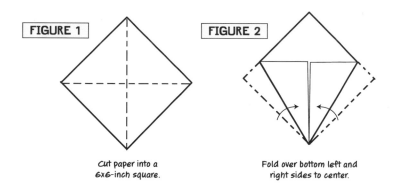

FIGURE 1

Cut paper into a
6x6-inch square.

FIGURE 2

Fold over bottom left and
right sides to center.

Next, fold the top corner down and to the right in the opposite direction of how you folded it to make **Figure 6**. Similarly, fold the bottom corner up but to the right, until the shape appears like the one in **Figure 8**.

Fold the bottom right corner to the center—it will fold the figure in half. See **Figure 9**. While you are folding it, shape the top right-pointing corners into a mouth shape by pushing the beak with your hand. See **Figure 10**. If necessary, fold and unfold the figure until this section resembles a mouth.

Last, draw eyes on both sides of the top portion of the figure. Now you can pull on the two bottom corners and the mouth will flap open and closed, as shown in **Figure 11**. If not, unfold the beak and refold it while adjusting it with your hand until the mouth moves properly.

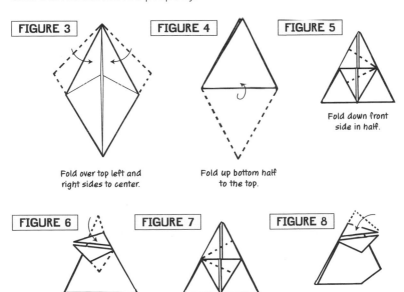

FIGURE 3

Fold over top left and right sides to center.

FIGURE 4

Fold up bottom half to the top.

FIGURE 5

Fold down front side in half.

FIGURE 6

Fold over front and back flaps to form shape above.

FIGURE 7

Unfold figure from shape in figure 6.

FIGURE 8

Fold up front flap and fold down back flap over to the right to form shape above.

FIGURE 9	**FIGURE 10**	**FIGURE 11**

Bend bottom right
section to center
and fold.

Form top sections
into mouth shape.
If necessary, unfold
and fold bottom section.

Pull bottom section
apart and the mouth
will open and close.

Sneaky Origami Animator

You can add motion to your origami designs, and other craft
creations, by making a Sneaky Origami Animator with everyday
objects.

What's Needed
Two large paper clips
Electrical tape
Five by three-inch piece of cardboard
Needle-nose pliers

What to Do
This project illustrates how to make a cam-crank toy to add
locomotion to your still figure designs. You can produce variations
on this design by using larger pieces of cardboard and stiff wire,
but it's recommended to make a simple version first. Later, you
can alter the size of the parts to produce your desired results.

First, bend one paper clip into the shape shown in **Figure 1**.
It will act as a mount for your origami figure.

Next, bend the second paper clip into the shape shown in
Figure 2. It will act as a cranking cam that will move the first
paper clip up and down. Wrap electrical tape around both
paper clips.

Poke holes in the cardboard at 1-inch, 2½-inch, and 4-inch
intervals, as shown in **Figure 3**. Then, stand the card along its
long side and fold it into a **U** shape.

Push the first paper clip into the center hole. Use pliers to
bend the top of the clip into a **C** shape so it will not fall through
the hole. See **Figures 4** and **5**.

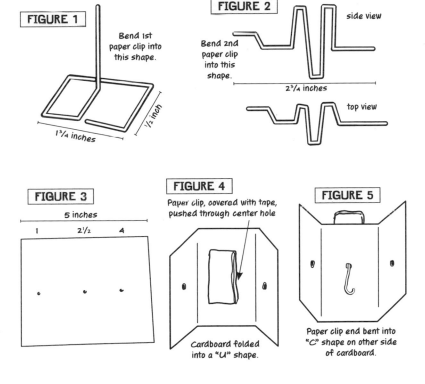

FIGURE 1

Bend 1st
paper clip into
this shape.

1¾ inches

½ inch

FIGURE 2

side view

Bend 2nd
paper clip
into this
shape.

2¾ inches

top view

FIGURE 3

5 inches

1   2½   4

FIGURE 4

Paper clip, covered with tape,
pushed through center hole

Cardboard folded
into a "U" shape.

FIGURE 5

Paper clip end bent into
"C" shape on other side
of cardboard.

Next, push the second paper clip into the side holes of the cardboard so it rests underneath the first paper clip, as shown in **Figure 6**. Apply tape to the bottom of the cardboard to keep its shape.

Last, turn the paper clip crank on the side of the Sneaky Origami Animator and the top paper clip will move up and down. See **Figure 7**. Since the first paper clip has an irregular shape, it acts as a cam mechanism and causes erratic movement on the other paper clip resting on it.

You can attach small paper figures to the top paper clip with tape. Experiment with an assortment of shapes for your paper clip cam (e.g., oval or triangular shapes) to produce a variety of motion effects. See the moving-arm figure in **Figure 8**.

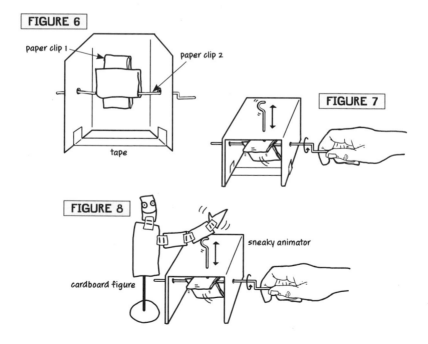

FIGURE 6

paper clip 1
paper clip 2
tape

FIGURE 7

FIGURE 8

cardboard figure
sneaky animator

Sneaky Solonoid

When electricity flows through a wire, it produces a magnetic field around it. If a magnet is brought near the wire, it will cause the wire to move toward it (or away, depending on its position). This project shows how to use this principle to create a Sneaky Solonoid—a mechanical switch activated by a magnetic coil, commonly used to open and close an electric circuit, a lock, or a valve.

What's Needed

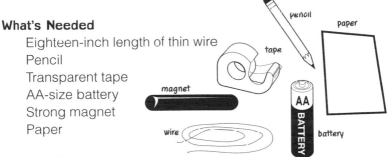

Eighteen-inch length of thin wire
Pencil
Transparent tape
AA-size battery
Strong magnet
Paper

What to Do

Strip the ends from the wire and wrap it ten turns around a pencil, using the center of the wire length to begin wrapping so that both ends are free. See **Figure 1**. Apply a small piece of tape to the wire coil to retain its shape, as shown in **Figure 2**.

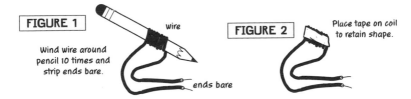

FIGURE 1
wire
Wind wire around pencil 10 times and strip ends bare.
ends bare

FIGURE 2
Place tape on coil to retain shape.

Tape one end of the wire to the AA battery's positive terminal and the other end to the side of the battery near the negative terminal. See **Figure 3**.

Place a magnet on the table and position the coil directly over it. When you press the wire on the battery's negative terminal, the wire coil will jump. If it moves toward the magnet, turn the magnet over. See **Figure 4**.

You've made a simple solonoid. Solonoids are used in many devices, such as an electric door lock, to allow a pushbutton to control motion or allow entry through the door. They are also used in radio control models to control the wings' ailerons and rudders for flight control.

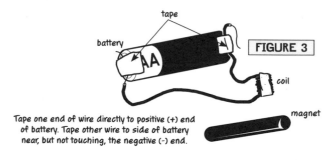

Tape one end of wire directly to positive (+) end of battery. Tape other wire to side of battery near, but not touching, the negative (-) end.

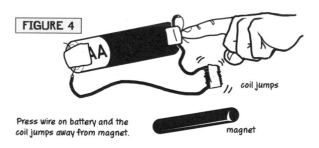

Press wire on battery and the coil jumps away from magnet.

Going Further

You can make the Sneaky Solonoid animate a small origami figure by taping it to the wire coil. See **Figure 5**.

To make a simple origami beetle, follow the directions below:

Start with a 2-inch square piece of thin paper, as shown in **Figure 6A**. Fold down the top corner to the bottom corner. See **Figure 6B**. Fold over the left and right corners close, but not all the way, to the center, as shown in **Figure 6C**. **Figure 6D** shows how to fold down the top and side corners to give the origami beetle a buglike appearance. Simply tape the beetle to the wire coil and have fun making it hop and dance.

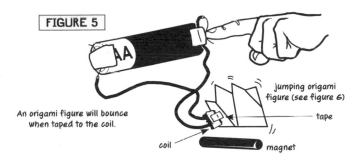

FIGURE 5

An origami figure will bounce when taped to the coil.

jumping origami figure (see figure 6)

tape

coil

magnet

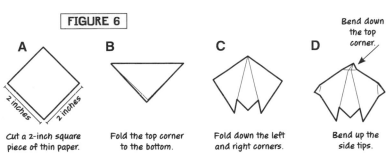

FIGURE 6

A	B	C	D
2 inches 2 inches			Bend down the top corner.
Cut a 2-inch square piece of thin paper.	Fold the top corner to the bottom.	Fold down the left and right corners.	Bend up the side tips.

The origami "beetle" is complete.

Sneaky Motor

When electrical current passes through a wire it produces a magnetic field that will attract some metals and other magnets. You can make a simple electromagnet with a battery, wire, and a nail or bolt.

When you press the wire ends against the battery, the current flow induces a magnetic field in the coil of wire. The nail amplifies the effect and you can attract small metallic objects or a magnet. Magnets have a north and south pole, and so does your electromagnet. If you turn the magnet over, it will be either attracted to or repelled by the nail.

Using this knowledge, you can create a Sneaky Motor using the same parts in a different way.

What's Needed

Transparent tape
Three D-size batteries, one of
    which is to be used as a mold
Cardboard
Two paper clips
Ten feet of insulated 14-gauge magnet wire
Strong disk-shaped or square magnet
Pliers

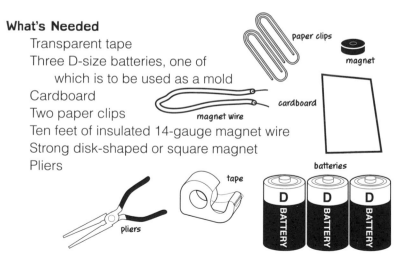

paper clips

magnet

cardboard

magnet wire

batteries

tape

pliers

What to Do

For this Sneaky Motor, you must use magnet wire found at electronic parts or hardware stores. Although it appears to be regular copper wire, it has copper-colored insulation that can be scraped off.

Tape two D-size batteries next to each other on to the cardboard as shown in **Figure 1**. Bend the two paper clips, as shown in **Figure 2**, and tape them to the ends of the batteries, perpendicular to the terminal ends so that they extend out in front of the batteries.

Next, wrap the wire around one D-size battery twelve times and wrap the ends to form a loop (making sure to leave a wire end free on each side of the coil), as shown in **Figures 3** and **4**. Then, very carefully use the rough inner surface of the pliers to scrape just one side of each end of the wires as shown in **Figure 5**. Do not scrape off the entire insulation, just one side (180 degrees).

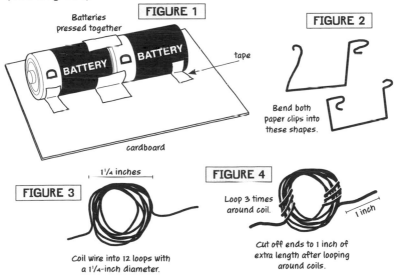

FIGURE 1

Batteries pressed together

BATTERY   BATTERY

tape

cardboard

FIGURE 2

Bend both paper clips into these shapes.

FIGURE 3

1¼ inches

Coil wire into 12 loops with a 1¼-inch diameter.

FIGURE 4

Loop 3 times around coil.

1 inch

Cut off ends to 1 inch of extra length after looping around coils.

Then, place the wire coil on the paper clip hooks and position the magnet below the wire coil. Finally, spin the coil, which should continue spinning on its own. If it does not, turn the coil around or reposition the magnet until it spins freely. See **Figure 6**.

When the coil is at rest, the insulation on the ends prevents battery power from flowing through it. When you spin the coil, the bare wire touches the paper clips and the battery current flows through the wire coil, inducing a magnetic field in it. This field repels the magnet and the coil turns. When the insulated side of the coil touches the paper clips, the current stops but the momentum keeps it going until the bare wire makes contact again.

You may wonder why you bare only one side of the coil ends. If the coil wire ends were completely bare, the coil would start to spin but then immediately stop because the coil's other side, or magnetic pole, would then attract the magnet. In addition, this constant current flow would cause the battery to heat and to rapidly lose power.

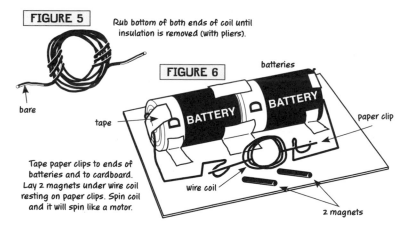

FIGURE 5

Rub bottom of both ends of coil until insulation is removed (with pliers).

bare

FIGURE 6

batteries

BATTERY

BATTERY

tape

paper clip

Tape paper clips to ends of batteries and to cardboard. Lay 2 magnets under wire coil resting on paper clips. Spin coil and it will spin like a motor.

wire coil

2 magnets

Sneaky Motor II

You've seen how a magnet will attract or repel a wire that has electrical current flowing through it. This project shows how to use this principle to create a Sneaky Motor. Although most motors produce circular motion, a motor is actually any device that uses electricity to obtain repetitive movement.

What's Needed

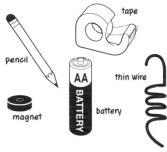

Eighteen-inch length of thin wire
Pencil
Transparent tape
Strong metallic disk magnet
AA-size battery

What to Do

This project uses the same design shown in the Sneaky Solonoid project, except the magnet is placed on the battery.

First, strip the ends from the wire, wrap it ten turns around a pencil leaving the wire ends free from the coil shape, and apply a small piece of tape to the wire coil to retain its shape, as shown in **Figure 1**.

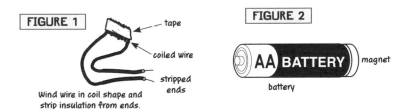

FIGURE 1
tape
coiled wire
stripped ends
Wind wire in coil shape and strip insulation from ends.

FIGURE 2
magnet
battery

Next, place the metallic disk magnet on the battery's negative terminal. See **Figure 2**. Then, tape one end of the wire coil to the battery's positive terminal. See **Figure 3**.

When you bend the wire coil so it rests on top of the magnet, it should start to move back and forth, as shown in **Figures 4** and **5**. (If it does not, turn over the magnet and test it again.)

How does it work? When the wire touches the magnet, electricity flows through it. It becomes magnetic and is repelled by the magnet. When it moves away from the magnet, it disconnects from the battery, loses it magnetic field, and falls back to its original position. It then reconnects to the battery through the metallic magnet, becomes magnetically charged again, and the cycle repeats.

For a more dramatic effect, bend the wire unto a **V** shape and tilt the battery downward. Ensure that the wire coil rests just above the magnet. When the wire is bent into a right angle, you will see the wire coil bounce up and down much farther. See **Figure 6**.

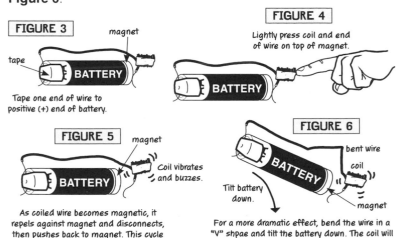

FIGURE 3

tape

magnet

BATTERY

Tape one end of wire to positive (+) end of battery.

FIGURE 4

Lightly press coil and end of wire on top of magnet.

BATTERY

FIGURE 5

magnet

BATTERY

Coil vibrates and buzzes.

As coiled wire becomes magnetic, it repels against magnet and disconnects, then pushes back to magnet. This cycle produces buzzing action.

FIGURE 6

bent wire

BATTERY

coil

Tilt battery down.

magnet

For a more dramatic effect, bend the wire in a "V" shpae and tilt the battery down. The coil will move a greater distance back and forth.

Sneaky Motor III

This project illustrates the versatility of the Sneaky Motor design but has a workaround in case you cannot locate a metallic disk magnet. A bonus application is included, using the motor to demonstrate how a radio control transmitter works.

What's Needed

Paper clip
Strong disk magnet
Pliers
Eighteen-inch length of thin wire
Pencil
Transparent tape
AA-size battery

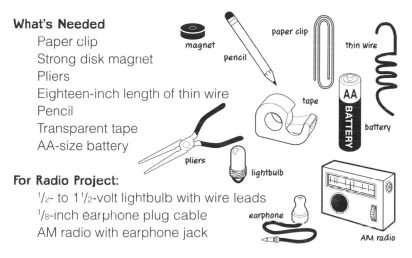

For Radio Project:

$1/2$- to $1 1/2$-volt lightbulb with wire leads
$1/8$-inch earphone plug cable
AM radio with earphone jack

What to Do

First, bend a paper clip into the shape shown in **Figure 1**. It should allow the magnet to slip in with a tight grip. See **Figure 2**.

FIGURE 1	FIGURE 2

Bend paper clip into a "C" shape.   Slide magnet between paper clip.

Note: If you cannot locate a small metallic disk magnet for your Sneaky Motor, a plain magnet can be used. You must add a small paper clip to act as a magnet holder. The paper clip also conducts electricity from the battery to the wire coil in this design.

Then, set up the battery as follows:

First, strip the ends from the wire, wrap it around a pencil ten times, and apply a small piece of tape to the wire coil to retain its shape. Then, tape one end of the wire coil to the battery's positive terminal, as shown in **Figure 3**.

When you bend the wire coil so it rests on top of the paper clip above the magnet, it should start to move back and forth. If it does not, turn over the magnet and test it again.

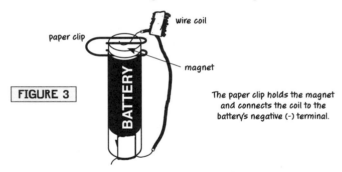

wire coil

paper clip

magnet

FIGURE 3

The paper clip holds the magnet and connects the coil to the battery's negative (-) terminal.

Bonus Sneaky Radio Control Demonstration

This project will take advantage of ordinary AM radio's sensitivity to electromagnetic interference. If you activate the Sneaky Motor near an AM radio that is tuned between stations with the volume turned up, you will hear a loud buzzing sound. When you move the motor away from the radio, the tone level decreases. See **Figure 4**.

The Sneaky Motor emits a magnetic field that is opening and closing. This produces a low-frequency interference signal, which the radio detects and amplifies. This signal can be used to power a small light connected to the radio's earphone jack.

Obtain a small lightbulb with leads from a single-cell flashlight or from an electronics parts store. The lightbulb should be rated to work with only 1$\frac{1}{2}$ volts of power. Connect the light leads to the $\frac{1}{8}$-inch earphone plug leads, as shown in **Figure 5**. If you tune the radio to an active station with the volume level high, the light should turn on when the earphone plug is plugged in.

For this project you must first tune the radio between stations, with the volume high. The light should not turn on. If it does, turn down the volume until it goes out. Then, bring the Sneaky Motor near the radio and activate it. This should produce enough interference that the light turns on. If not, adjust the volume level until it does. See **Figure 6**.

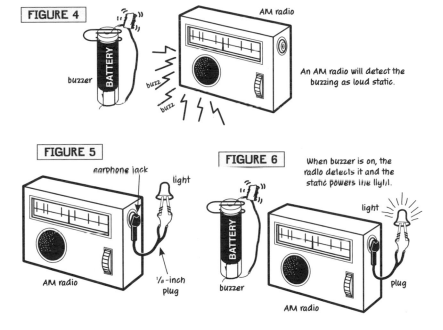

FIGURE 4

buzzer
BATTERY

AM radio

An AM radio will detect the buzzing as loud static.

FIGURE 5

earphone jack
light
AM radio
$\frac{1}{8}$-inch plug

FIGURE 6

When buzzer is on, the radio detects it and the static powers the light.

buzzer
BATTERY
light
plug
AM radio

Sneaky Motor IV

You can also make a motor using a battery, magnet, and piece of stiff copper wire to produce a spiraling circular motion around the battery.

What's Needed

Needle-nose pliers
Six-inch length of stiff copper wire
AA-size battery
Two strong disk magnets
approximately ³/₄ inch in diameter

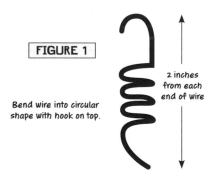

copper wire

magnets

battery

pliers

What to Do

This project uses the same design shown in the Sneaky Solonoid project, except that two magnets are placed on the battery's negative (–) terminal.

Note: In this design, the magnets must be larger in diameter than the battery.

FIGURE 1

Bend wire into circular shape with hook on top.

2 inches from each end of wire

First, strip the insulation off the wire. Bend the top of the wire into a hook shape. Press the tip into a sharp point with the pliers. Wrap the wire in a spiral form that will fit around the body of the battery as shown in **Figure 1**. The wire should be just loose enough to not contact the battery case.

Next, place two disk magnets on the battery's negative terminal. See **Figure 2**. Adjust the shape of the wire so the top rests on the center positive (+) terminal and the bottom just touches the side of the magnet, as shown in **Figure 3**. The length from the tip of the top hook and the bottom of the wire should be 2 inches.

Once the wire makes contact with the top battery terminal, it will spin around. See **Figure 4**. If it does not, carefully bend and adjust the wire so that it is free to move and make contact properly.

You can also turn the magnets over to make the wire spin in the other direction.

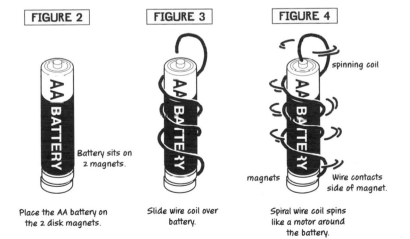

FIGURE 2

Battery sits on 2 magnets.

Place the AA battery on the 2 disk magnets.

FIGURE 3

Slide wire coil over battery.

FIGURE 4

spinning coil

magnets

Wire contacts side of magnet.

Spiral wire coil spins like a motor around the battery.

How It Works

When the wire touches the battery's top positive terminal and the side of the magnet, electricity flows through it. The wire becomes magnetic and is repelled by the two disk magnets. When the wire moves away from the magnet, it disconnects from the battery and loses its magnetic field. It falls back to its original position and contacts the side of the magnet. Then, it connects to the battery via the magnet and becomes magnetically charged again, and the cycle repeats.

Since the wire coil is suspended by its sharp tip on top of the battery's positive terminal, when it repels from and returns to the magnet, it rotates slightly. The cycle occurs so quickly that it generates a circular motor motion.

Sneaky Motor V

Another motor can be put together using a battery and two disk magnets. This time, a small pointed screw and a piece of thin stranded wire are added to the mix.

What's Needed

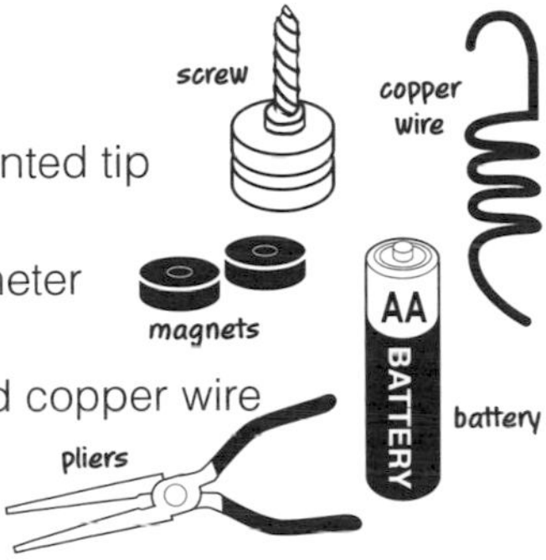

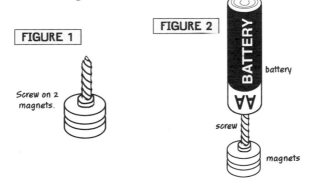

- ³/₄-inch or longer screw with a pointed tip
- Two strong disk magnets approximately ³/₄ inch in diameter
- Needle-nose pliers
- Three-inch length of thin-stranded copper wire
- AA-size battery

What to Do

Place the base of the screw on the two magnets, as shown in **Figure 1**. Then, point the tip of the screw at the positive (+) battery terminal until it sticks to it because of magnetic attraction. See **Figure 2**.

FIGURE 1

Screw on 2 magnets.

FIGURE 2

battery

screw

magnets

Then, strip the insulation off the stranded wire using the pliers. Next, hold the battery, hanging screw, and magnets with your thumb and middle finger. Hold one end of the wire to the battery's negative (−) terminal with your forefinger, as shown in **Figure 3**.

To start the Sneaky Motor turning, press the other end of the wire to the top edge of the topmost magnet, using your other hand. See **Figure 4**. The magnets and screw should start spinning and will continue even when you disconnect the wire. If you turn the magnets over, they will spin in the other direction.

How It Works

When the wire touches the battery's top negative terminal and the edge of the magnet, electricity flows through it. The wire becomes magnetic, causing the magnets to repel it. When this happens, the wire loses its magnetic field and the magnets fall back to their original position of resting on the wire. Then, the wire reconnects to the battery, through the magnets, and becomes magnetically charged again, thus repeating the cycle.

The cycle of movement makes the magnets rotate slightly, because they pivot on the battery terminal via the point of the screw.

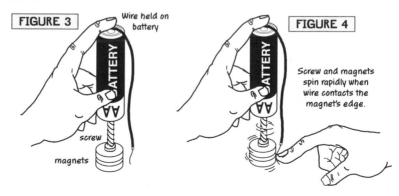

FIGURE 3

Wire held on battery

BATTERY

screw

magnets

FIGURE 4

BATTERY

Screw and magnets spin rapidly when wire contacts the magnet's edge.

Sneaky Sugar Glass

When you see a character in a TV show or movie crash through a window, it's not really glass they are breaking. Special effects men use a sheet of clear substance that's actually made of sugar!

You can make your own fake glass for models and hobby projects like they do in the movies. All you need are a few common kitchen items.

What's Needed
Butter
Nonstick pan or baking sheet
One cup of sugar
Nonstick frying pan
One tablespoon of water

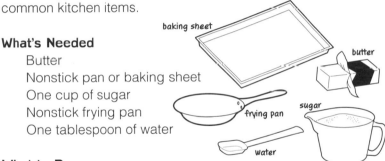

baking sheet

butter

sugar

frying pan

water

What to Do
First, spread a thin layer of butter on the surface of the baking sheet and let it cool for one hour in the refrigerator. Then, pour a cup of sugar into the frying pan, add the water, and place the pan on a stove-top burner. Turn the heat on low. See **Figures 1** and **2**.

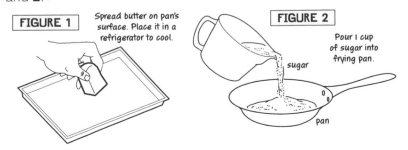

FIGURE 1 Spread butter on pan's surface. Place it in a refrigerator to cool.

FIGURE 2 Pour 1 cup of sugar into frying pan.

sugar

pan

Next, stir the sugar continually so it will not burn. It will liquefy when heated. See **Figures 3** and **4**. When the sugar is completely liquefied but before it starts to turn brown, remove the baking sheet from the refrigerator and pour the sugar onto it, as shown in **Figure 5**. (Be sure to turn off the heat, and to allow the pan to cool on an unheated burner before you wash it.)

Let the sugar cool and you will have a sheet of fake glass that you can use for hobby models and other projects. See **Figure 6**.

FIGURE 3

FIGURE 4

Stir the sugar to prevent burning.

Add 1 tablespoon of water at low temperature.

pan

FIGURE 5

Once the sugar liquefies but before it turns brown, pour it onto the cooled pan.

FIGURE 6

After the sugar cools and hardens, remove it carefully from the tray.

Sneaky Calculator

You can make a simple-to-make toy for young children just learning addition and subtraction. You just need a couple of discarded Styrofoam cups and a pen. Plus, you'll prevent the cups from needlessly filling up landfill space.

What's Needed

    Two white, rimmed Styrofoam cups
    Pen
    Ruler

pen

ruler

Styrofoam cups

What to Do

First, obtain two cups that have a lip at the top. Place one cup into the other as shown in **Figure 1**.

Next, using the pen and ruler, draw a plus sign (+) on the lip of the top cup and the numbers 1 through 20 exactly ¼ inch apart. Similarly, draw a negative sign (–) on the rim of the bottom cup and the numbers 1 through 20 exactly ¼ inch apart. See **Figure 2**.

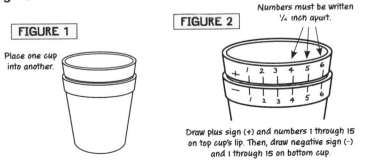

FIGURE 1

Place one cup into another.

FIGURE 2

Numbers must be written ¼ inch apart.

+ 1 2 3 4 5 6
– 1 2 3 4 5 6

Draw plus sign (+) and numbers 1 through 15 on top cup's lip. Then, draw negative sign (–) and 1 through 15 on bottom cup.

How to Add Numbers

Following the arrows in the example shown in **Figure 3**, start with a number on the bottom cup, in this case the number 5. Turn the top cup so the plus sign (+) is above the number 5 on the bottom cup. Then, select a number on the top cup that you want to add to 5. In this instance, it is the number 3. Look at the number below 3, on the bottom cup, and the answer is 8.

You can repeat this process with any number adding up to 20. Select a number on the lower cup, align the plus sign above it, and then on the top cup select a number to add. You will see the sum immediately below the number you added.

How to Subtract Numbers

See the example problem in **Figure 4** and follow the arrows. Start with a number on the bottom cup, in this case the number 10. Turn the top cup so the number you wish to subtract is above the first number you selected on the bottom cup. In this instance it is the number 7. Then, look at the plus sign (+) on the top cup. Below the symbol, on the bottom cup, is the answer: the number 3.

You can repeat this process with any number up to 20. Select a number on the lower cup and turn the cup to align it with the number on the top cup that you wish to subtract. Look at the plus sign on the top cup and you'll see the answer below it on the lower cup.

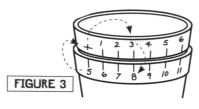

FIGURE 3

To add, start with bottom cup's number; match with (+) on top cup and number to add. The sum is below that number on the lower cup. Example: 5 (+) 3 = 8

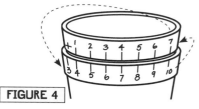

FIGURE 4

To subtract, select a number on the bottom cup, in this example 10. Align it with the number to subtract, which is 7. The answer is below the (+) sign: 3.

Sneaky School Quiz Tester 1

You can add a little fun to the chore of studying for a test by making a sneaky quiz tester. This 3-D model complements written material and adds a little fun in the process.

What's Needed

Two disk magnets
Scissors
White cardboard box
Pencil
Tape

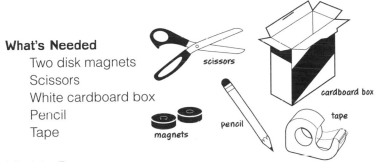

scissors

cardboard box

tape

pencil

magnets

What to Do

First, test the two magnets to see which ends are north and which are south. When magnets stick together, the north end of one is attracted to the south end of the other. Indicate both magnets' north and south ends with a marker.

Next, cut the cardboard into the shape illustrated (an unfolded box) in **Figure 1**, being careful to follow the exact dimensions shown. Fold the segments into 1¼-inch square sections, as shown. Tape a magnet, north side up, to one of the square sections.

On the second cutout, tape another magnet in place with its south side up. See **Figure 2**.

Fold each cutout into a box shape, fitting the tabs into the slots. Write, with a pencil, a sample quiz question on the surface of one box, on the outside of the section that has the magnet taped to its inner side. See **Figure 3**. Write an assortment of answers on the second box, one answer per side, placing the correct answer on the section whose magnet is attached to its inner surface.

As shown in **Figure 4**, when the two boxes are brought together, they will attract each other only when the question and the correct answer are aligned.

You can erase and write additional quiz questions and answers on the front of the boxes as desired.

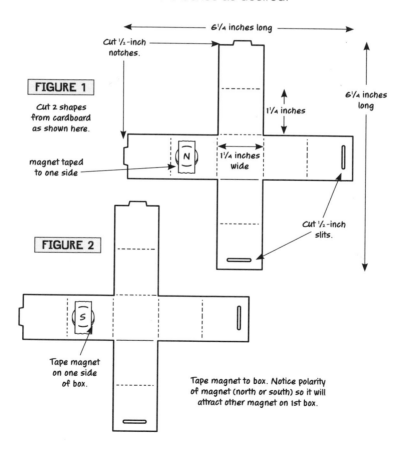

6¼ inches long

Cut ½-inch notches.

FIGURE 1

Cut 2 shapes from cardboard as shown here.

magnet taped to one side

6¼ inches long

1¼ inches

1¼ inches wide

N

FIGURE 2

Cut ½-inch slits.

Tape magnet on one side of box.

S

Tape magnet to box. Notice polarity of magnet (north or south) so it will attract other magnet on 1st box.

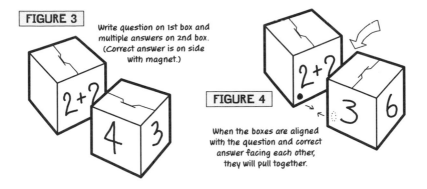

FIGURE 3

Write question on 1st box and multiple answers on 2nd box. (Correct answer is on side with magnet.)

FIGURE 4

When the boxes are aligned with the question and correct answer facing each other, they will pull together.

Sneaky School Quiz Tester II

Here's another Sneaky Quiz Tester you can build with everyday things. Its larger size allows for more questions and answers to be selected, as well as greater visibility, for a group of students.

What's Needed

Cardboard box
Scissors
Tape
Pliers
1½-volt lightbulb
Ten paper clips
Five feet of insulated wire
AA-size battery
Paper
Pencil

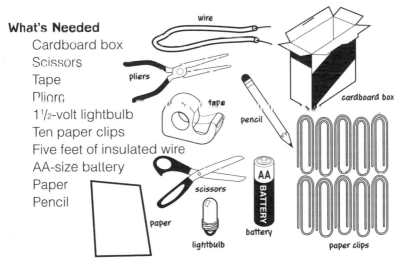

What to Do

You can use a cardboard box from a food product for this project. An empty cereal box is perfect. Simply unfold it, cut off the top flap and back, and turn it inside out. Tape the corners together, as shown in **Figure 1**, so it stands upright.

Next, using the scissors, carefully puncture five small holes on each side of the box and two at the top. Also cut a small hole at the top of the box for the bulb, as shown in **Figure 2**. Then, push the bulb through the top hole. Also, unbend ten paper clips so you can push them through the back of the box. See **Figure 3**.

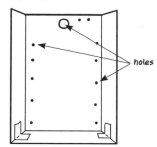

FIGURE 2

Cut holes into box front—small ones 5 on each side and 2 at the top, plus one in the center for the lightbulb.

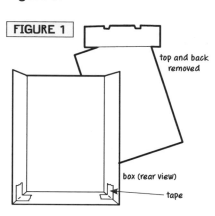

FIGURE 1

top and back removed

box (rear view)

tape

Dismantle box, turn inside out, and remove top flaps and back side. Tape bottom together so it stands upright.

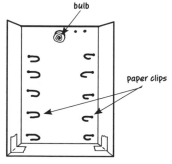

FIGURE 3

Push bulb and paper clips into holes from front of box.

bulb

paper clips

Cut a 3-inch length of wire and two 10-inch lengths. Strip the insulation off the ends of the wires.

Tape the AA battery to the top of the box and secure the 3-inch length of wire from the battery around the side of the lightbulb's base. Tape one of the 10-inch wires to the bottom of the bulb and push its other end through one of the two small holes at the top. Tape the other 10-inch wire to the remaining battery terminal and push its other end through the other small hole at the top. See **Figure 4**. When the two wires touch, the lightbulb should turn on. If it doesn't, check the connections to all of the parts and test it again.

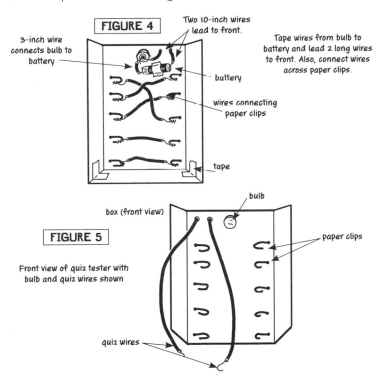

FIGURE 4

3-inch wire connects bulb to battery

Two 10-inch wires lead to front.

Tape wires from bulb to battery and lead 2 long wires to front. Also, connect wires across paper clips.

battery

wires connecting paper clips

tape

FIGURE 5

Front view of quiz tester with bulb and quiz wires shown

box (front view)

bulb

paper clips

quiz wires

Cut five 7-inch lengths from the remaining wire and strip the insulation from their ends. Wrap the wires around the paper clips on the box, running them side to side in various patterns (straight and crisscross), as shown in **Figure 4**. When the two 10-inch quiz wires make contact with the proper paper clips in the front of the Quiz Tester (in the example shown in **Figure 6**, 1 + 4 = 5), it will make a complete circuit and turn on the light. When you look from the front of the Quiz Tester box, the bulb and 10-inch wires should be protruding from the back to the front. The 10-inch wires will be used to connect to a paper clip to each side of the box and light the bulb, indicating a correct answer. See **Figure 5**.

Cut a piece of paper so it will fit between the columns of paper clips on the front of the box. Write some math questions on the left side and some answers on the right with a pencil. Be sure to use the correct pattern of wire connections on the back as a guide. See **Figure 4** as an example. When the two 10-inch-long quiz wires touch the top left-side paper clip and the second to top paper clip on the right side, respectively, the light will turn on to indicate the correct answer, as shown in **Figure 6**.

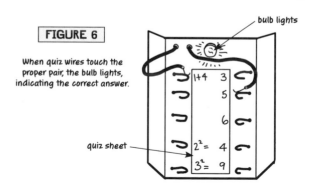

| FIGURE 6 |

When quiz wires touch the proper pair, the bulb lights, indicating the correct answer.

bulb lights

quiz sheet

Sneaky Robot

Robots are fascinating because of their utility and resemblance to humans. But you don't have to buy an expensive and complicated kit when you can make a Sneaky Robot from everyday things.

In the projects that follow, you'll learn how to use discarded toy cars, cardboard, and other items to make a modular "trashformer" that's easy to construct and disassemble. If desired, you can go all the way and make your own giant 6-foot sneakbot out of parts found around the house.

Chassis and Body

What's Needed

Motorized toy car, wire- or radio-controlled
Plastic ice trays or small
    parts box
Pringles containers (chip cans)
Two wire garment hangers
Double-stick Velcro pads
Transparent tape
Scissors
Pliers
Optional:
Tablecloth
Plastic dining tray

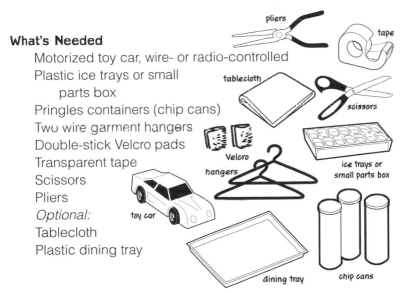

pliers
tape
tablecloth
scissors
Velcro
hangers
toy car
ice trays or small parts box
chip cans
dining tray

What to Do

The simplest robot can be constructed using an inexpensive radio-controlled car as its base. The car should include a full-function remote control. Small, cheap radio-control cars that are always in motion and only go in reverse when you press the remote's single button are not recommended for this robot project. A medium-to-large car model with a full-function remote control should be used to provide ample torque. (Of course, if you do not want mobility for your robot, then the car is unnecessary.) The robot's body is mounted on the car's chassis with Velcro pads, allowing for easy construction and disassembly.

Sneaky Robots can be assembled using just two basic parts: plastic ice trays and Pringles chip cans. Ice trays provide an excellent modular, low-cost horizontal base that can support the upper parts. They allow you to easily increase the height of the robot by placing one section on top of another.

Pringles containers, which hereon we'll refer to as chip cans, are great for adding vertical height to the robot's body. Like ice trays, they, too, are modular and, with their plastic cap, allow for easy construction and disassembly.

Double-stick Velcro pads, tape, and wire hangers are used for connecting the parts and to keep the body rigid. See how to fit the materials together in **Figures 1** through **4**.

Besides being a fun toy, a Sneaky Robot can be used as a mobile TV dinner tray, as shown in **Figure 5**.

When making a tall Sneaky Robot, it's important to stabilize the lowest ice tray to the car with strong rubber bands and to use three chip cans, in a tripod arrangement, to prevent the robot from tipping over. See **Figure 6**.

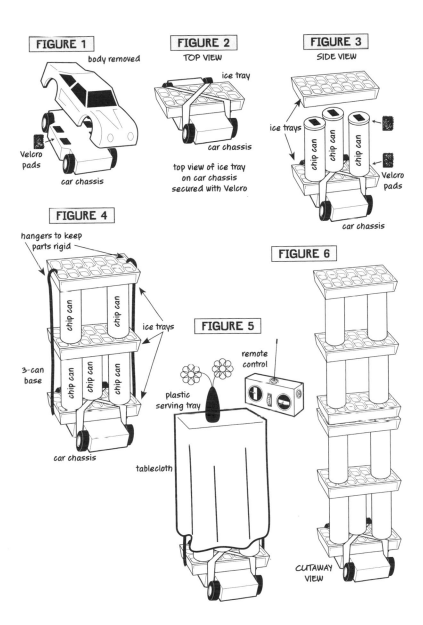

FIGURE 1

body removed

Velcro pads

car chassis

FIGURE 2

TOP VIEW

ice tray

car chassis

top view of ice tray
on car chassis
secured with Velcro

FIGURE 3

SIDE VIEW

ice trays

chip can

chip can

chip can

Velcro pads

car chassis

FIGURE 4

hangers to keep
parts rigid

chip can

chip can

chip can

chip can

chip can

chip can

ice trays

3-can base

car chassis

FIGURE 5

remote control

plastic serving tray

flowers

tablecloth

FIGURE 6

CUTAWAY VIEW

Body Decoration and Accessories

After designing and assembling the basic robot chassis and frame, you'll want to decorate it so that it resembles a cybernetic being. You probably already have plenty of materials in the house that can decorate your robot. Additional inexpensive materials and useful accessories can be obtained from discarded toys and local thrift stores.

Note: The suggested parts list below will depend on the extent of your robot design.

What's Needed (Suggested)

Cloth material
Plastic tablecloth
Decorative mask
Foil material (from emergency blanket)
Slinky Jr.
Small flexible-neck flashlights
Juice bottle
Wire garment hangers
Electrical wire
Double-stick Velcro pads
Glue
Transparent tape
Scissors
Pliers
Markers and pens
Small magnets
Voice memo recorder
Blinking LED party lights
Small LCD digital clock
Calculator

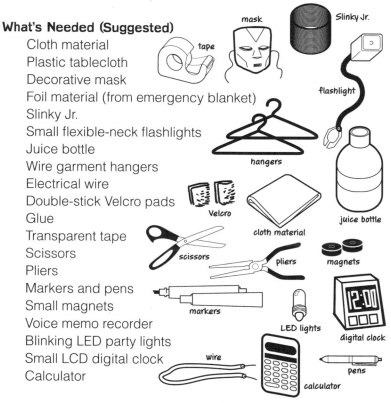

Walkie-talkies
Toy metal detector
Personal battery-powered fan
CDs
Antennas
Umbrella
Pie pans
Circuit board from toy
TV dinner tray
Mini radio
Vacuum cleaner hose
Plastic cups
Plastic tray

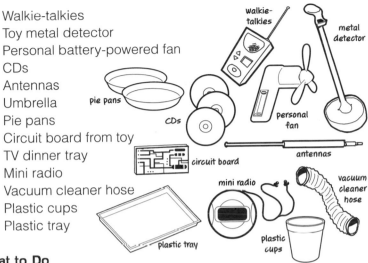

What to Do

Figure 1 illustrates several robot head designs. Or, you can substitute an available decorative mask at the top of the robot.

The robot's arms can be constructed using wire hangers covered with cloth material, plastic vacuum cleaner hoses, or Slinky Jr. coils. Attach strong magnets or clamps so the robot can transport objects. See **Figure 2**.

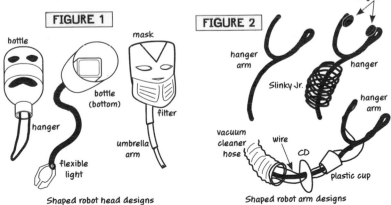

Shaped robot head designs

Shaped robot arm designs

You can buy inexpensive decorative accessories at dollar stores, and mount such devices as LED lights, an LCD clock, or a calculator keypad in or on the robot body, as desired. If your robot design uses a soft body covering, such as foil material, mount the accessory parts with double-stick Velcro strips directly on one of the upper trays. You can cut holes in the body covering and apply tape around the decorative objects as needed. See **Figure 3**.

Why not use the mobility of your Sneaky Robot to do some surveillance or search for hidden treasures? You can easily attach a couple of accessories you probably already have for added fun.

A walkie-talkie, compact radio, or a small toy metal detector can be useful additions, as shown in **Figure 4**. The robot's walkie-talkie can be used to transmit your voice from a remote location. Or, if you'd rather listen in, place the button in its TRANSMIT mode (if the button will not stay in the TRANSMIT mode, you can secure it with tape). In this way, you can send the robot to a remote location and monitor the environment from afar.

Similarly, you can attach a compact metal detector, the type with a removable handle, to the lower part of the robot chassis with Velcro strips, to enable you to walk along without holding the handle, as shown in **Figure 5**.

Going Further

Your Sneaky Robot has virtually limitless accessory and utility options. For added convenience, you may want to remount the robot's main ON/OFF switch to a more accessible location.

Consider adding sound-effect devices from toys, plus radio control receivers, obtained from micro radio-control cars, to control these optional devices.

If you build more than one robot, you can stage friendly battles by outfitting them with foam or plastic toy bats and

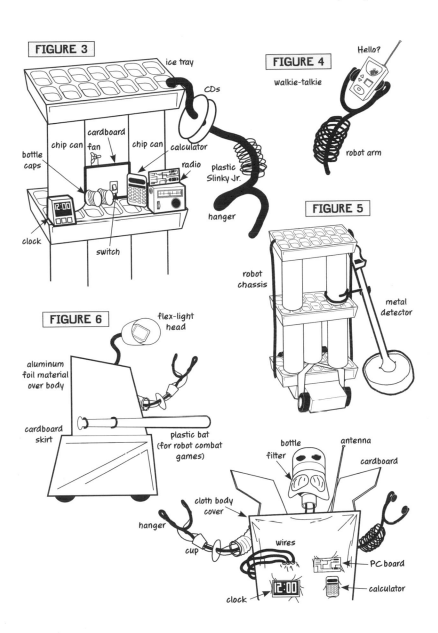

FIGURE 3

ice tray

CDs

cardboard fan

chip can

chip can

calculator

bottle caps

radio

plastic Slinky Jr.

clock

switch

hanger

FIGURE 4

Hello?

walkie-talkie

robot arm

FIGURE 5

robot chassis

metal detector

FIGURE 6

flex-light head

aluminum foil material over body

cardboard skirt

plastic bat (for robot combat games)

bottle filter

antenna

cardboard

cloth body cover

hanger

cup

wires

clock

PC board

calculator

light sabers, as shown in **Figure 6**. Be sure to use radio-controlled cars with different transmission frequencies to avoid interference.

For versatility, design a robot chestplate that can be easily attached and removed with Velcro strips. You can easily alter the robot's style to fit your tastes or a special event (such as Halloween, a birthday, or a competition). Simply cut a piece of cardboard slightly smaller than the upper body area on the robot and, using Velcro strips (or glue), apply spare electronic parts from old computers and toys such as wire cables, printed circuit boards, LEDs, voice memo recorders, digital clocks, and calculators to the cardboard for a high-tech look. See **Figure 7**. When you've completed the chestplate, attach Velcro to the back and simply press it onto the Velcro strips on the front of the robot, as shown in **Figure 8**.

Sneaky Robot arms can be made with stiff wire or a clothes hanger. Bend the hanger until it resembles the shape shown in **Figure 9**. One side will clip onto the ice tray and the other end forms a claw shape. Decorate the robot arm with found items like old CDs or a Slinky Jr. toy, and secure the parts with tape. See **Figure 10**. Last, bend the end of the hanger until it clips securely to the edge of the ice tray and secure it firmly with tape. If desired, small magnets can be attached to the end of the robot arms so it can hang on to lightweight metallic objects. See **Figure 11**.

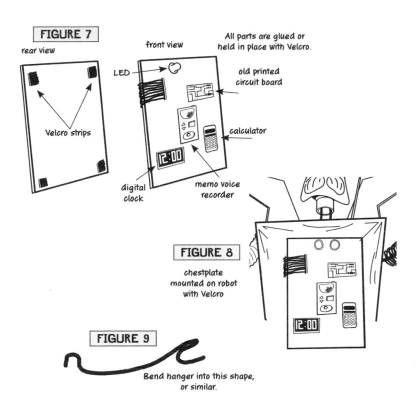

FIGURE 7

rear view

front view

All parts are glued or held in place with Velcro.

LED

old printed circuit board

calculator

Velcro strips

digital clock

memo voice recorder

FIGURE 8

chestplate mounted on robot with Velcro

FIGURE 9

Bend hanger into this shape, or similar.

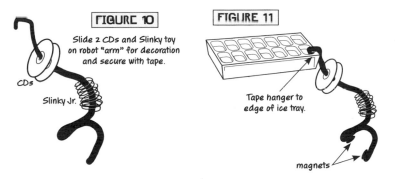

FIGURE 10

Slide 2 CDs and Slinky toy on robot "arm" for decoration and secure with tape.

CDs

Slinky Jr.

FIGURE 11

Tape hanger to edge of ice tray.

magnets

Sneaky 6-Foot Sneakbot

To really make a big impression you can create your own giant sneakbot easily enough by adding another level or two of chip cans and ice trays.

What's Needed

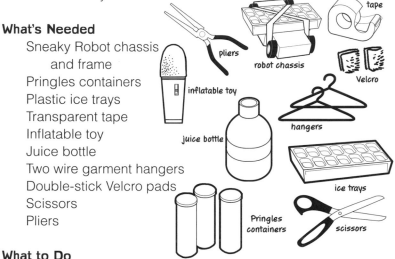

Sneaky Robot chassis
   and frame
Pringles containers
Plastic ice trays
Transparent tape
Inflatable toy
Juice bottle
Two wire garment hangers
Double-stick Velcro pads
Scissors
Pliers

tape

pliers

robot chassis

Velcro

inflatable toy

hangers

juice bottle

ice trays

Pringles containers

scissors

What to Do

First, assemble the chassis and body from the Sneaky Robot project.

Then, assemble an additional level or two of chip can and ice tray segments, as shown in the previous robot project, and place the bottommost ice tray of that portion atop the ice tray that completes the lower level of the robot, as shown in **Figure 1**. Secure the ice trays with tape.

To increase the robot's height without adding additional ice tray/chip can segments, you can attach an inflatable toy, with mask, to act as the head. Your lower body decorations, accessories, and arms can be mounted to the upper sections, as shown in **Figure 2**.

Note: If necessary, use a three-can tripod arrangement and add weight to the lowest segments, to lower the center of gravity and prevent the robot from tipping over when it accelerates. Also, add more wire hangers to the side of the ice trays as needed, to keep the upper segments rigid.

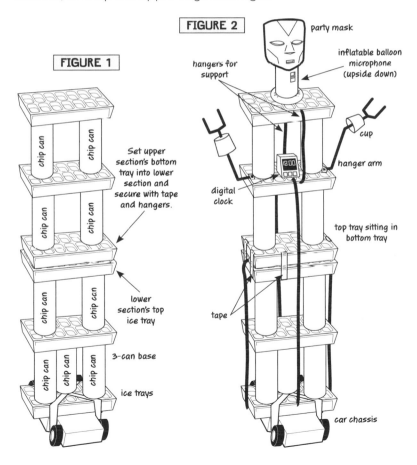

FIGURE 1

chip can

Set upper section's bottom tray into lower section and secure with tape and hangers.

lower section's top ice tray

3-can base

ice trays

FIGURE 2

party mask

inflatable balloon microphone (upside down)

hangers for support

cup

hanger arm

digital clock

top tray sitting in bottom tray

tape

car chassis

PART III

Sneaky Energy Projects and Simulations

Energy affects everybody. We depend on it for transportation, industry, and to power our homes. Yet the average person doesn't fully comprehend the ever-increasing ways that energy is obtained, produced, and distributed. This part of *Sneakiest Uses for Everyday Things* includes background details, experiments, and simulations to help you understand your options for choosing cleaner, renewable energy.

Do you know how oil is refined and how biofuels can substitute for gasoline and diesel fuel? If you're curious about how a hybrid car can utilize normally wasted energy during braking or whether hydrogen fuel cells will soon power vehicles, or want details about atomic energy, then this part of the book is for you. Here, you'll learn the basic techniques used to obtain energy from coal, oil, gas, the sun, wind, and water and from the atom. The nuclear power simulation project, made with cardboard and paper clips, can also be adapted to demonstrate other energy-related projects.

Whether you want to know energy theory or want a practical guide to making unique energy-related science simulations, the following projects will expand your knowledge of energy in a fun and interesting way, to help you make more informed choices that protect our planet.

Energy Fundamentals

Energy is what makes things change or move. It is found in many forms, including heat, chemical, light, electrical, and mechanical energy.

Kinetic energy is the energy in moving things. Energy that can be stored for later use is called *potential energy.* Gases, solids, and chemicals can all store potential energy that may be released later in a variety of ways.

For instance, when certain substances, such as coal, are burned, the process releases energy in the form of heat. In a coal-fired electrical power plant, the heat that the released energy produces is used to boil water into steam, which in turn propels turbine blades to power an electrical generator. See **Figure 1**.

Food, oil, and batteries have potential energy stored within their chemicals. Springs and rubber bands do, as well. They can be wound up to store *strain energy* for later use.

Energy can be converted from one form or another for practical use. Common energy conversions take place all the time, all around you. For example:

- The sun provides energy for plants to make food. This food is stored as *chemical energy.* When animals eat plants, they convert the chemical energy into motion and heat.
- Chemical energy is stored in consumer batteries, where it is converted into electricity. The electricity is changed into heat, light, motion, or sound, depending on whether the batteries are in a flashlight, toy, radio, or other device.

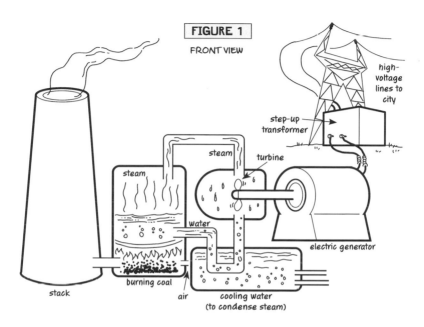

FIGURE 1

FRONT VIEW

high-voltage lines to city

step-up transformer

steam

turbine

steam

water

electric generator

burning coal

stack

air

cooling water
(to condense steam)

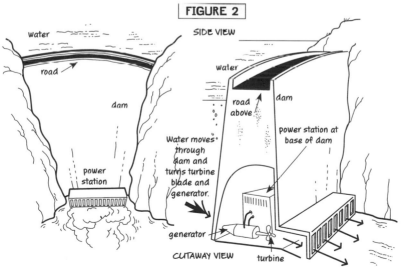

FIGURE 2

SIDE VIEW

water

road

dam

power station

water

road above

dam

power station at base of dam

Water moves through dam and turns turbine blade and generator.

generator

CUTAWAY VIEW

turbine

- Hydroelectric power plants use water at a high elevation to fall on turbine blades, which turn electrical generators. As shown in **Figure 2**, water, blocked by a dam, flows through a penstock channel where it eventually reaches a turbine. The rushing water spins the turbine blades and provides mechanical energy to an electrical generator.
- Wood, oil, and coal store energy from the sun as chemical energy. In the case of gas, oil, and coal, they are burned to release chemical energy in the form of heat. Geothermal power plants use underground pockets of steam to power turbines.

Electrical power stations have large water, gas, or steam turbines that turn electrical generators. An electrical generator diagram is shown in **Figure 3**. To reduce energy loss while traveling over long-distance power lines, step-up transformers increase the voltage level from about 15,000 to 20,000 volts, to several hundred thousand volts. Electric power substations, located near cities, use distribution transformers to step down the voltage to about 7,200 volts. Line transformers, near homes and businesses, step down the voltage level to 240 volts.

Wires leading from line transformers can be tapped to produce 120 volts, for most needs, or 240 volts for heavy-duty appliances such as washers and dryers. See **Figure 4**.

The next project illustrates an easy-to-make multistage example of energy storage and conversion.

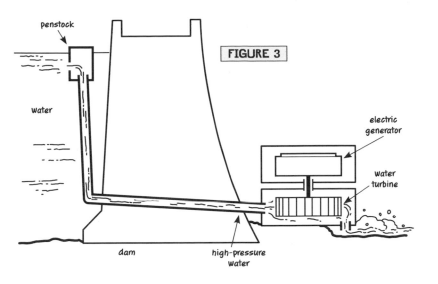

penstock

FIGURE 3

water

electric generator

water turbine

dam

high-pressure water

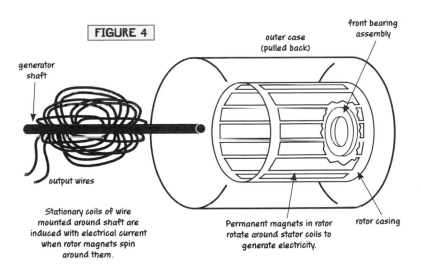

front bearing assembly

FIGURE 4

outer case (pulled back)

generator shaft

output wires

Stationary coils of wire mounted around shaft are induced with electrical current when rotor magnets spin around them.

Permanent magnets in rotor rotate around stator coils to generate electricity.

rotor casing

FIGURE 5

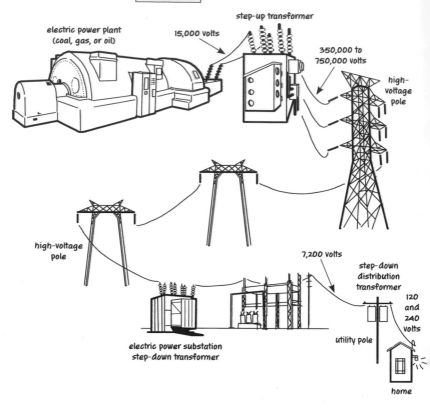

Energy Conversion and Storage Demonstration

If you tire of constantly manually rewinding the rubber band–powered planes or other toy models, you can use everyday things to make an automatic rewinder. This project demonstrates how one form of energy can be converted and stored in another form.

The chemical energy in a battery is converted into electrical energy that is converted, by a toy car's motor, into mechanical energy. This mechanical energy is then used to wind a rubber band taut and is stored as potential energy.

What's Needed

Large paper clip
Toy car
Rubber band–operated plane

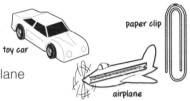

paper clip

toy car

airplane

What to Do

This project requires a medium-size toy car, not the small ones found in dollar stores. Smaller model motors do not generate enough power to wind a rubber band tightly.

First, bend the large paper clip into the **V** shape shown in **Figure 1**. Most toy cars have holes in the wheels that make it easy to push the paper clip through, as shown in **Figure 2**. Once it's in position, spread the ends of the paper clip apart slightly to secure it in place. See **Figure 3**.

FIGURE 1

Bend paper clip into "V" shape.

Then, place the paper clip ends on each side of the model plane's propeller and turn on the car. The car motor will spin the propeller and the motor will spin the blades, to wind the rubber band as shown in **Figure 4**.

When disconnected from the paper clips, the rubber band releases its stored energy. See **Figure 5**.

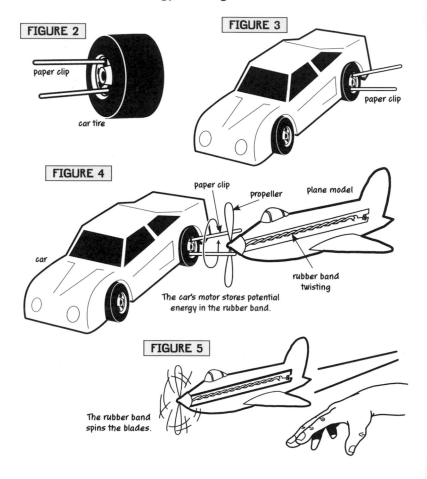

FIGURE 2

paper clip

car tire

FIGURE 3

paper clip

FIGURE 4

paper clip   propeller   plane model

car

rubber band twisting

The car's motor stores potential energy in the rubber band.

FIGURE 5

The rubber band spins the blades.

Solar Power Demonstrations

In the following projects we will take advantage of the sun's radiation by using its heat, as well as utilizing solar cells to generate electricity.

Sneaky Solar Cooker

What's Needed
- Aluminum foil
- Transparent tape
- Bowl
- Large paper clip
- Potato
- Rock

What to Do

Wrap the aluminum foil into a cone shape and tape it to the inside of the bowl as shown in **Figure 1**.

Bend the paper clip into a **C** shape, as shown in **Figure 2**. Tear away a small piece of foil in the center of the bowl and tape the paper clip to the bowl.

To test your solar cooker, stick a small potato on the end of the paper clip, as shown in **Figure 3**. Place the bowl in direct sunlight for one to two hours and move it occasionally to keep it in line with the sun until the potato is cooked, as shown in **Figure 4**. You now have a free Sneaky Solar Cooker.

FIGURE 1

aluminum foil

bowl

tape

Wrap foil in bowl, with it
taped over mouth.

FIGURE 2

Bend paper clip like this.

FIGURE 3

Tape paper clip to
bottom center of bowl.

paper clip

tape

FIGURE 4

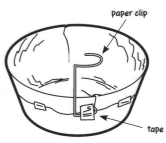

potato

rock

Bowl tilted
toward sun

Solar Power Generator

Solar cells convert light from the sun into electricity. A
photovoltaic (PV) cell is a semiconductor that needs a little
energy to allow electron flow between its N- and P-type layers.
Solar cells have a protective cover, an antireflective coating, and
electrical contacts that collect photons, particles of solar energy,
and transfer them into electric current. See **Figure 1**.

Solar cells can be removed from small toys and calculators
or purchased separately from electronic parts supply houses
and hobby stores.

You can demonstrate how solar power can be used to
power devices by connecting a solar cell to a miniature radio-
controlled car.

What's Needed

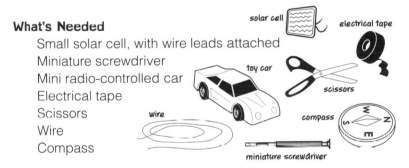

solar cell
electrical tape
toy car
scissors
wire
compass
miniature screwdriver

    Small solar cell, with wire leads attached
    Miniature screwdriver
    Mini radio-controlled car
    Electrical tape
    Scissors
    Wire
    Compass

What to Do

First, obtain a small solar cell with wire leads already attached
(so you do not have to solder).

Next, carefully remove the body from the mini radio-
controlled car. Most models allow you to pry off the body from
the chassis with a miniature flat-bladed screwdriver. The motor
can usually be lifted out of the chassis once the motor cover (if
found) is pried open as shown in **Figure 2**.

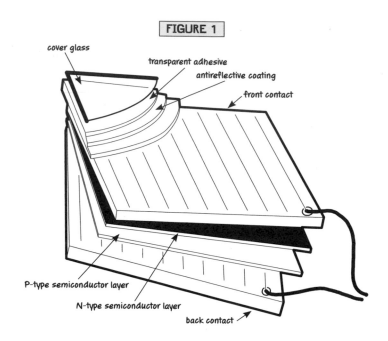

FIGURE 1

cover glass

transparent adhesive

antireflective coating

front contact

P-type semiconductor layer

N-type semiconductor layer

back contact

Connect the solar cell wires to the terminals of the motor with tape, as shown in **Figure 3**. If you only see one terminal or wire, the motor casing is its negative (–) terminal. Place the solar cell and motor under a bright light or in the sun and it should start to spin.

The car should move on its own when exposed to sunlight and, possibly, a bright room lamp. See **Figure 4**.

Wire that is connected to the solar cell can move a compass needle when it's wrapped around a compass. See **Figure 5**.

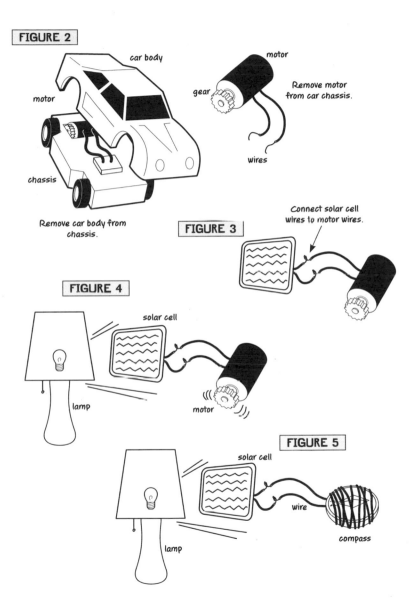

FIGURE 2

car body

motor

motor

gear

Remove motor from car chassis.

chassis

wires

Remove car body from chassis.

Connect solar cell wires to motor wires.

FIGURE 3

FIGURE 4

solar cell

lamp

motor

FIGURE 5

solar cell

lamp

wire

compass

Sneaky Oil Refinery Demonstration

Over 60 percent of the world's energy is derived from oil and natural gas. Much as time and pressure can turn coal into diamonds, organic remains from plants and animals were converted to oil deposits by millions of years of heat and pressure.

Basically, when oil is discovered, it is brought to the surface, gas and water are removed, and what remains is then pumped through pipelines to a refinery. An oil rig at sea and an oil refinery are shown in **Figures 1** and **2**. This project will illustrate how an oil refinery converts crude oil into useful products, including gasoline.

In a refinery, crude oil is pumped into a large furnace and boiled into a gas. It is then pumped into a distillation tower to condense back into different liquid substances at various temperatures. You've witnessed evidence of condensation on a cold glass of liquid, or on grass in the early morning in the form of dew droplets. The water in the air turns into a liquid when it comes in contact with a cooler surface.

A refinery's distillation tower uses the same principle to gather different types of oil products as the heated oil condenses. **Figure 3** shows the distillation tower, which has multiple levels of saucer-shaped cool surfaces against which the oil will form condensation (liquid). This condensation drips into trays and flows to gathering tanks. The higher tanks gather oil that is cooler than what is produced in the lower ones. By this process, the key ingredients for various petroleum products, including bitumen, diesel, gasoline, kerosene, and plastics, are obtained.

You can demonstrate how a refinery works, using common items found in every kitchen.

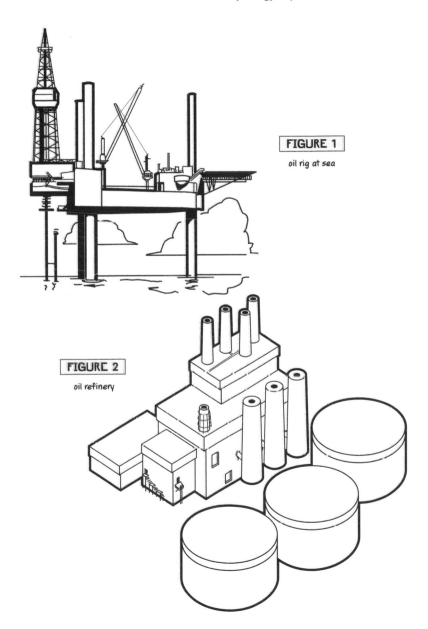

FIGURE 1

oil rig at sea

FIGURE 2

oil refinery

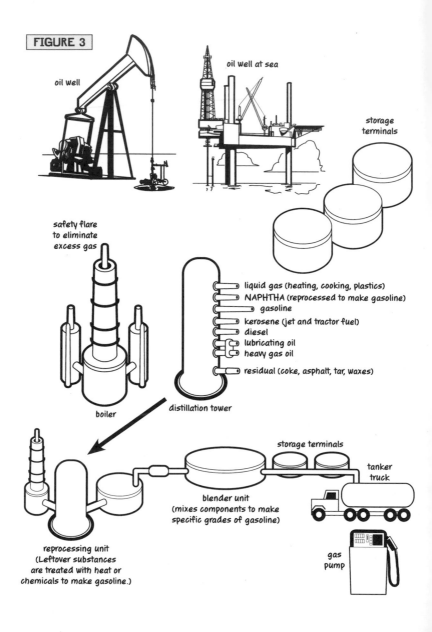

FIGURE 3

oil well

oil well at sea

storage terminals

safety flare to eliminate excess gas

liquid gas (heating, cooking, plastics)
NAPHTHA (reprocessed to make gasoline)
gasoline
kerosene (jet and tractor fuel)
diesel
lubricating oil
heavy gas oil
residual (coke, asphalt, tar, waxes)

boiler

distillation tower

storage terminals

tanker truck

blender unit (mixes components to make specific grades of gasoline)

reprocessing unit (Leftover substances are treated with heat or chemicals to make gasoline.)

gas pump

What's Needed

Teakettle filled with water
Bowl
Metal pan
Ice cubes
Oven mitt

What to Do

Bring water to a boil in the teakettle. Place a bowl near the stove a few inches away from the kettle, as shown in **Figure 1**.

Next, fill the metal pan with ice cubes. See **Figure 2**. With an oven mitt, hold the pan over the bowl, near the kettle's spout, as shown in **Figure 3**.

When the steam gathers on the pan's bottom surface, which is cooled by the ice cubes, it condenses (turns into a liquid), and drips into the bowl.

FIGURE 1

FIGURE 2

Place ice cubes on tray.

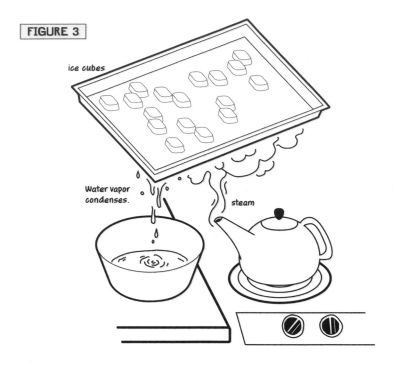

FIGURE 3

ice cubes

Water vapor
condenses.

steam

Biofuels
Biofuels are liquid fuels derived from crops. They include
methanol (wood alcohol), ethanol (grain alcohol), and biodiesel.

Biodiesel
Rudolf Diesel made diesel engines in 1895 that could run on
peanut oil. Diesel engines differ from gasoline engines because
of their higher compression ratio.

Currently, in the United States, diesel cars account for less
than 4 percent of the market while in Europe over 50 percent
of passenger vehicles are diesel powered. A diesel engine
produces higher torque at lower RPMs (rotations per minute)

and gets better gas mileage, compared with its gasoline counterpart.

Standard gasoline engines use a spark plug to ignite the air-fuel mixture as shown in **Figure 1**.

In a diesel engine, the pistons compress the air-fuel mixture in the cylinder so much that the extreme heat ignites it without requiring a spark plug. See **Figure 2**.

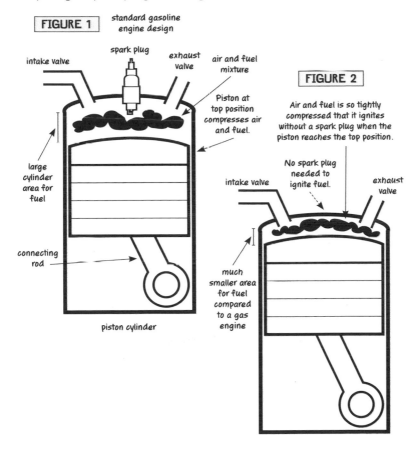

FIGURE 1 standard gasoline engine design

spark plug

intake valve

exhaust valve

air and fuel mixture

Piston at top position compresses air and fuel.

large cylinder area for fuel

connecting rod

piston cylinder

FIGURE 2

Air and fuel is so tightly compressed that it ignites without a spark plug when the piston reaches the top position.

No spark plug needed to ignite fuel.

intake valve

exhaust valve

much smaller area for fuel compared to a gas engine

All diesel engines can use biodiesel fuel if it is heated and filtered properly. Biodiesel can be made, via a chemical process, from recycled cooking oil, animal fats, soy, corn, sunflower seeds, canola, peanuts, mustard seeds, or cottonseeds. Solar energy, combined with water and carbon dioxide, provides the stored energy captured by feedstock.

Even ordinary vegetable oil or filtered cooking oil from restaurants can power biodiesel-ready vehicles.

Since the crops use carbon dioxide from the atmosphere in their energy absorption process, they are virtually a carbon-neutral source of fuel. When the vehicle's exhaust emits carbon dioxide, it's absorbed by crops and the biodiesel carbon cycle continues, as shown in **Figure 3**.

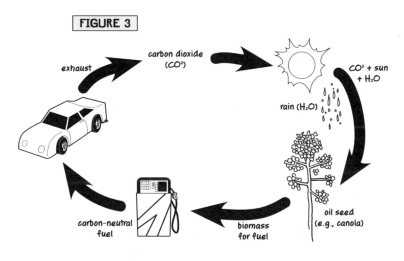

FIGURE 3

exhaust

carbon dioxide
(CO_2)

CO_2 + sun
+ H_2O

rain (H_2O)

oil seed
(e.g., canola)

biomass
for fuel

carbon-neutral
fuel

BIODIESEL CARBON CYCLE

Sneaky Ethanol Demonstration

Ethanol has been used to power vehicles since the early twentieth century—Henry Ford had ethanol-fueled Model T vehicles. Ethanol (specifically, E85—a mixture of 85 percent ethanol and 15 percent gasoline) vehicles have been available for consumers since 1992.

Ethanol can also be produced from biomass feedstocks, including corn stalks, grasses, paper, wood wastes (e.g., wood chips and sawdust), and green wastes (e.g., vegetable and fruit wastes, leaves, and grass clippings).

Figure 1 illustrates the basic ethanol production process. Corn is crushed and mixed with water. It is heated and mixed with enzymes to convert its starch into sugar. Then, it is fermented with yeast to make alcohol. To boost the alcohol content, the mixture is boiled and then dehydrated.

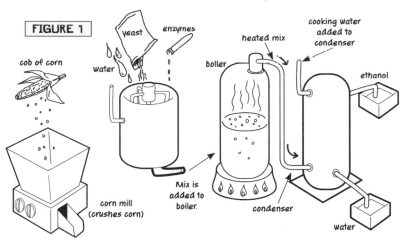

FIGURE 1

cob of corn

corn mill (crushes corn)

water

yeast

enzymes

Mix is added to boiler.

heated mix

boiler

cooking water added to condenser

ethanol

condenser

water

Ethanol emits cleaner emissions (carbon dioxide or CO_2, carbon monoxide, and particulate emissions) compared with gasoline and diesel fuel.

This project will enable you to demonstrate how sugar breaks down into ethyl alcohol, ethanol, and carbon dioxide.

What's Needed

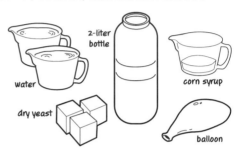

Two cups of water
5 cubes of dry yeast
Two-liter bottle
¹/₄ cup of corn syrup
Balloon

2-liter bottle

water

corn syrup

dry yeast

balloon

What to Do

First, pour the 2 cups of water and 5 cubes of yeast into the bottle and mix them by shaking the bottle for one minute. See **Figure 2**.

Then, pour the ¹/₄ cup of corn syrup in the bottle and shake it for a minute. Wrap the lip of the balloon over the mouth of the bottle, as shown in **Figure 3**. Let the bottle sit, and monitor the liquid and the balloon every two hours.

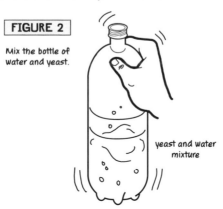

FIGURE 2

Mix the bottle of water and yeast.

yeast and water mixture

You will first see some bubbles appear on the surface of the mixture, and eventually the balloon will inflate. Fermentation is taking place. This is the process by which the yeast breaks down the sugar in the corn syrup into ethyl alcohol (ethanol) and carbon dioxide (which rises and inflates the balloon). See **Figure 4**.

You can also perform this demonstration by substituting a cola drink or table sugar for the corn syrup. Try testing all three mixtures with three separate bottles and note the amount of time for bubbles to form and the rate of inflation of the balloon.

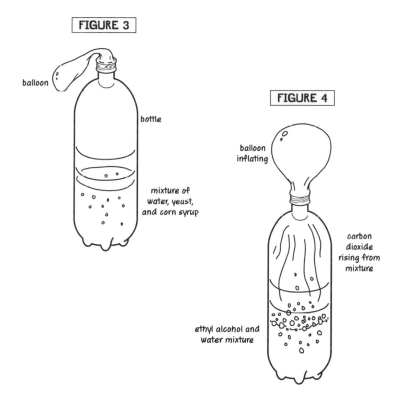

FIGURE 3

balloon

bottle

mixture of
water, yeast,
and corn syrup

FIGURE 4

balloon
inflating

carbon
dioxide
rising from
mixture

ethyl alcohol and
water mixture

Sneaky Electrical Generator

New energy sources are being found and refined every day, and you can demonstrate how industry, smaller businesses, and individuals take advantage of various forms of alternate energy sources. This project illustrates three methods that harness the power of wind, water, and steam to produce electricity.

When a wire moves near a magnet, an electrical current is induced. Using this knowledge, you can create a Sneaky Electrical Generator with a toy motor.

What's Needed

> Three large paper clips
> Electrical tape
> Toy car motor
> Pliers
> Voltmeter
> Wire (optional)

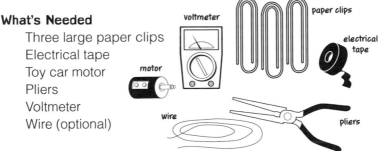

What to Do

First, bend the three paper clips into the shapes shown in **Figure 1**. Paper clip 1 will act as a hand crank. The other two paper clips will act as propeller blades.

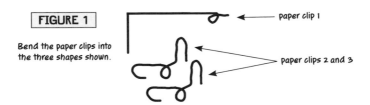

FIGURE 1

Bend the paper clips into the three shapes shown.

paper clip 1

paper clips 2 and 3

Next, wrap electrical tape around the shaft of the toy car motor. See **Figure 2**.

If the motor does not have wires on its two terminals, tape two 4-inch lengths of wire to them with tape.

Then, attach the first paper clip to the motor shaft and press it tight with pliers. Place the voltmeter on its lowest direct current (DC) setting and wrap the motor wires around its probes. Cranking the motor should cause the voltmeter to indicate a current has been generated, as shown in **Figure 3**.

Next, remove the first paper clip and press the other two paper clips onto the motor shaft as shown in **Figure 4**. Reshape the first paper clip to resemble the other two and press it onto the motor shaft also. See **Figure 5**.

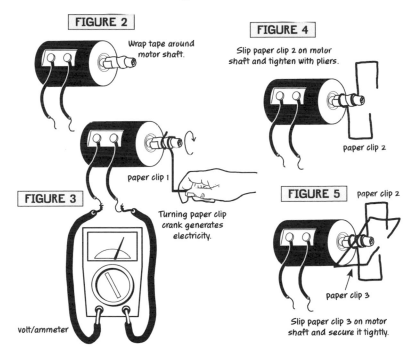

| FIGURE 2 |
Wrap tape around motor shaft.

| FIGURE 4 |
Slip paper clip 2 on motor shaft and tighten with pliers.

paper clip 2

paper clip 1

| FIGURE 3 |
Turning paper clip crank generates electricity.

volt/ammeter

| FIGURE 5 | paper clip 2

paper clip 3

Slip paper clip 3 on motor shaft and secure it tightly.

Apply tape to all three paper clips to form propeller blades, as shown in **Figure 6**.

If you blow on the propeller or use a small hair dryer on it, the blades will turn and you will be harnessing wind power to generate electricity.

You can carefully hold the motor blades near a teakettle spout to harness steam power or place the propeller under a faucet's stream of running water to harness hydro power as shown in **Figure 7**.

Note: If you have a personal battery-powered fan, you can connect it to the voltmeter and spin its blades with your fingers to attain the same effect. See **Figure 8**.

Figure 9 illustrates the internal parts of a wind turbine. Multiple wind turbines, called a wind farm, are shown in **Figure 10**.

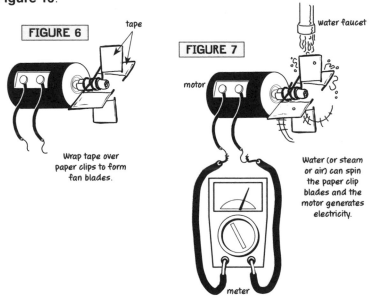

FIGURE 6

tape

Wrap tape over paper clips to form fan blades.

FIGURE 7

water faucet

motor

meter

Water (or steam or air) can spin the paper clip blades and the motor generates electricity.

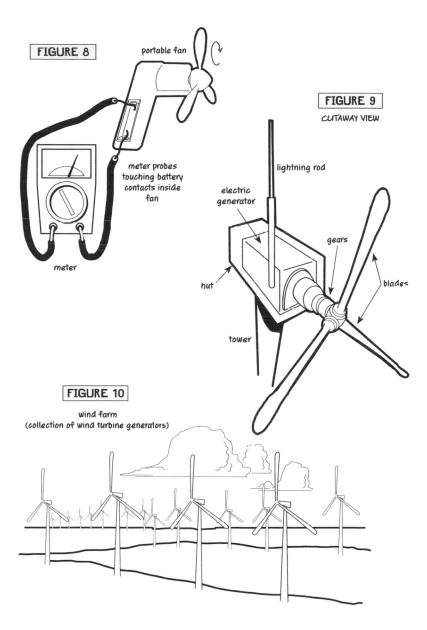

FIGURE 8

portable fan

meter probes
touching battery
contacts inside
fan

meter

FIGURE 9

CUTAWAY VIEW

lightning rod

electric
generator

gears

blades

hut

tower

FIGURE 10

wind farm
(collection of wind turbine generators)

Sneaky Hybrid Car Demonstration

Hybrid cars utilize two different methods of power—usually a gas combustion engine and an electrical motor—to power the vehicle. Depending on the design, a hybrid car can use one type of power for initial movement at low speeds and then another form of propulsion at higher speed, to optimize gas savings. Some hybrid models use both types of power simultaneously to complement each other.

For instance, a Toyota Prius hybrid initially uses an electric motor for low speeds, usually under 10 miles per hour, and switches to its gasoline engine for high-speed operation.

During braking, standard vehicles use mechanical pressure against brake drums or disks to slow the vehicle. Energy is lost as heat during this process. The Prius has another power-saving technology: a second, smaller motor/generator uses energy normally lost to heat during braking, to recharge its battery or act as a motor itself to add power to the engine's output. See **Figure 1**.

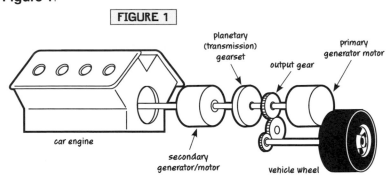

FIGURE 1

This project will show how to make a hybrid car that stores energy for use when the primary source is not active.

What's Needed

Rubber band
Two paper clips
Wire or thread spool
Transparent tape
1 large paper clip
Toy wire- or radio-controlled car

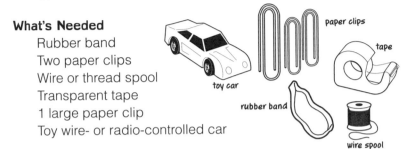

toy car

paper clips

tape

rubber band

wire spool

What to Do

First, thread the rubber band into the opening of a regular paper clip and back through the hole on the other end of the rubber band. Pull tightly until a knot is formed, as shown in **Figure 2**. Push the rubber band through the spool and use tape to secure the paper clip to the outside. See **Figure 3**.

Bend another regular paper clip into a **V** shape, as shown in **Figure 4**. Slip the loose end of the rubber band onto the middle of the **V**-shaped paper clip. See **Figure 5**.

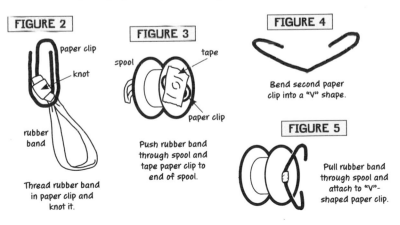

FIGURE 2

paper clip

knot

rubber band

Thread rubber band in paper clip and knot it.

FIGURE 3

spool

tape

paper clip

Push rubber band through spool and tape paper clip to end of spool.

FIGURE 4

Bend second paper clip into a "V" shape.

FIGURE 5

Pull rubber band through spool and attach to "V"-shaped paper clip.

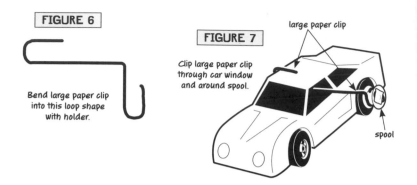

FIGURE 6

Bend large paper clip into this loop shape with holder.

FIGURE 7

Clip large paper clip through car window and around spool.

large paper clip

spool

Next, bend the large paper clip so that one side has a round hook to hold the spool (see **Figure 6**) and the other end will fit through the toy car window. **Figure 7** shows how to mount the spool onto the large paper clip and secure it to the car.

Next, bend the large paper clip so the spool will touch the floor surface and spin when the car moves on the floor. Using the remote control, run the toy car in circles on the floor at least five times around the room. Carefully lift the car while holding the spool. Pull the spool off the large paper clip and set it on the floor. It will spin on its own because the rubber band was wound by the toy car's movement.

Sneaky Hydrogen Power Demonstration

Hydrogen is an energy carrier, not an energy source. In the future, hydrogen fuel cells will be virtually emission-free forms of energy storage devices.

Fuel cells use a chemical reaction to produce electricity by combining hydrogen and oxygen. A diagram of a polymer electrolyte membrane (PEM) fuel cell is shown in **Figure 1**. Hydrogen enters the fuel cell's anode, where its electrons and protons are separated. The protons pass through the PEM while the electrons are forced to take an external route, which makes electricity. Oxygen is fed into the cathode side and combines with the protons and electrons to form water. The cycle repeats and produces an electrical current. See **Figure 2**. This process is called *electrolysis*.

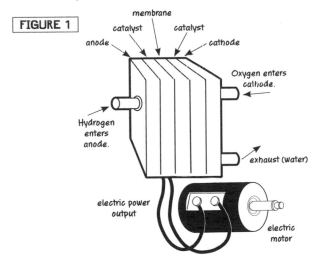

FIGURE 1

membrane
catalyst   catalyst
anode   cathode

Oxygen enters cathode.

Hydrogen enters anode.

exhaust (water)

electric power output

electric motor

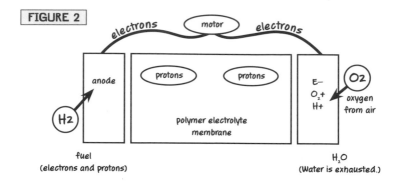

FIGURE 2

electrons   motor   electrons

anode

H2

protons   protons

polymer electrolyte
membrane

E−
O_2+
H+

O2

oxygen
from air

fuel
(electrons and protons)

H_2O
(Water is exhausted.)

You can demonstrate this process by separating water (H_2O, composed of hydrogen and oxygen) into its two elements with electricity.

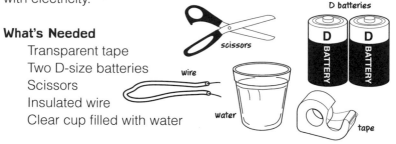

scissors

D batteries

D BATTERY   D BATTERY

wire

water

tape

What's Needed

Transparent tape
Two D-size batteries
Scissors
Insulated wire
Clear cup filled with water

What to Do

Tape the two D-size batteries together with one positive end connected to the negative end of the other. See **Figure 3**.

Cut two pieces of insulated wire and strip the insulation from both ends of them. Tape the wires to the ends of the battery terminals, as shown in **Figure 4**.

Next, place both of the free wire ends in the cup of water. See **Figure 5**. You should soon see bubbles appear on the ends of the wire lead. One of them will have about twice as many bubbles. This is hydrogen gas separating from the oxygen, as shown in **Figure 6**.

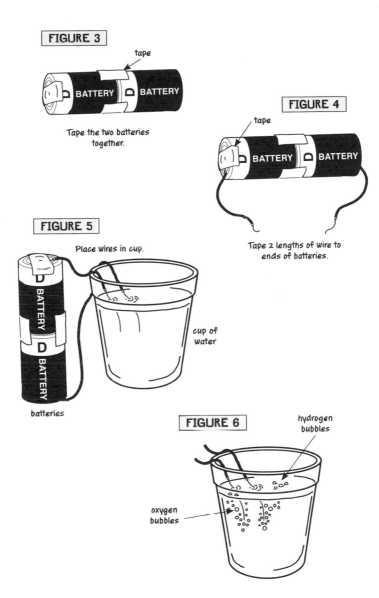

FIGURE 3

tape

BATTERY | BATTERY

Tape the two batteries
together.

FIGURE 4

tape

BATTERY | BATTERY

Tape 2 lengths of wire to
ends of batteries.

FIGURE 5

Place wires in cup.

BATTERY

BATTERY

cup of
water

batteries

FIGURE 6

hydrogen
bubbles

oxygen
bubbles

Sneaky Atomic Fundamentals Simulation

Nuclear Power

Radioactive material, like uranium, must be located, mined, and enriched before it can be put to use in nuclear power plants. The following projects provide experiments and simulations for unique science projects.

Nuclear Fission Simulation

Elements are the basic building blocks of matter in the universe and are made from just one type of atom.

Atoms are the building blocks of an element. A group of atoms bound together is called a *molecule*. Compounds are two or more different type of atoms bound together. For instance, water (H_2O) consists of two hydrogen atoms and one oxygen atom.

Although atoms are the smallest bit of a pure substance, atoms are made up of still smaller particles. They include *neutrons* and *protons* in its center (or nucleus) with *electrons* circling around them. See **Figure 1**.

Note: An element's *atomic number* is the number of protons in the nucleus.

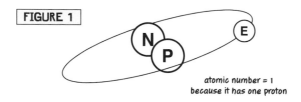

FIGURE 1

atomic number = 1
because it has one proton

Atoms of the same substance that have a different number of neutrons are called *isotopes*. For example, most hydrogen atoms have just one electron and one proton in their nucleus. A rare form of hydrogen that instead has one proton and one neutron in its nucleus is called *deuterium*. Another hydrogen isotope, which has one proton and two neutrons, is called *tritium*. See **Figure 2**.

Nuclear fission is the process of releasing nuclear energy by splitting the nucleus of uranium or plutonium atoms. Most uranium is the type called U-238 because it has 92 protons and 146 neutrons in its nucleus, for a total of 238 nuclear particles. It is radioactive but, when bombarded by neutrons, it absorbs them and the nucleus does not split. This type does not produce a fission chain reaction on its own.

An isotope of uranium that has three fewer neutrons (143) in its nucleus is called U-235. It is very rare and volatile. U-235 atoms will easily produce a fission chain reaction because there are already stray neutrons in the air. When a stray neutron flies into the nucleus of a U-235 atom and splits it, two neutrons fly out. These two neutrons split more atoms, releasing four more neutrons, and so on, starting a chain reaction that produces tremendous heat energy. See **Figure 3**.

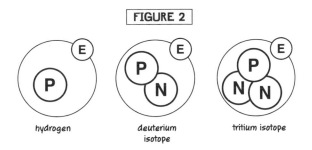

FIGURE 2

hydrogen   deuterium isotope   tritium isotope

Hydrogen atoms and their isotopes

fission reaction

| FIGURE 3 |

Heat is emitted.

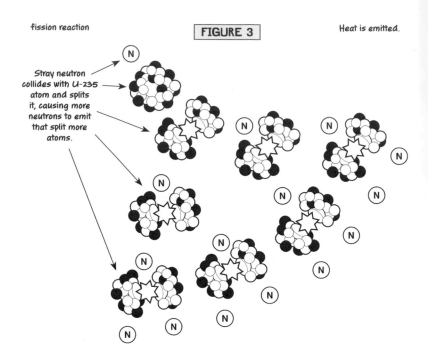

Stray neutron collides with U-235 atom and splits it, causing more neutrons to emit that split more atoms.

You can make a simple simulation of nuclear fission, using 3 by 5-inch cards. Draw illustrations of a single neutron, then an atom splitting and emitting more neutrons and more atoms splitting on the next cards, as shown in **Figure 4**.

When you push over the first card, which represents a stray neutron, it causes the other cards to fall. This chain reaction represents the splitting uranium 235 atoms, whose ejected neutrons split more atoms. See **Figure 5**.

Uranium enrichment is the process of separating U-235 isotopes from the more prevalent U-238. Two methods are widely used to enrich uranium: gas diffusion and centrifuge diffusion.

FIGURE 4

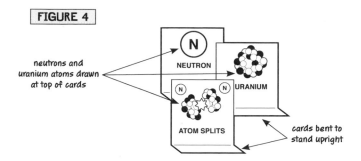

neutrons and uranium atoms drawn at top of cards

cards bent to stand upright

FIGURE 5

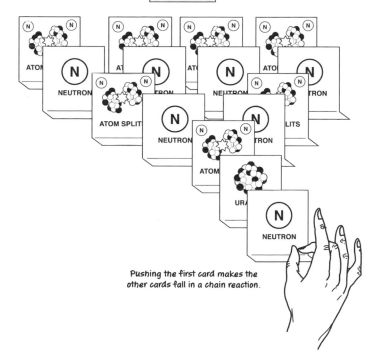

Pushing the first card makes the other cards fall in a chain reaction.

Gas diffusion consists of using a filter, like a kitchen strainer, to block larger particles from going through.

Centrifuge diffusion spins a substance to separate the heavier material, the way a clothes washer extracts water from garments during its spin cycle.

Gas Diffusion Enrichment Simulation

The gas diffusion method mixes uranium with fluoride to create uranium fluoride gas. This gas is pumped into filters that block the heavier uranium 238, with its three extra neutrons, but allow the lighter U-235 atoms through.

You can demonstrate this isotope-filtering process, using common household items.

What's Needed
 Scissors
 Waxed paper
 Bowl
 Tape
 Needle
 Large spoon
 Salt
 Flour

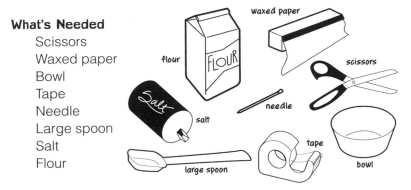

What to Do
First, cut a piece of waxed paper that will cover the top of the bowl and affix it with tape so that it stays in place, as shown in **Figure 1**. Carefully using the needle, puncture about thirty holes in the waxed paper. See **Figure 2**.

Then, use the spoon to pour equal parts of salt and flour on the waxed paper, as shown in **Figure 3**. (The salt will represent a U-238 atom; and the flour, a U-235 atom.)

Rub the mixture around on the surface with the bottom of the spoon. See **Figure 4**. Remove the rubber band and waxed paper, and check the bowl. It should have more flour, which is finer and lighter than the salt, as shown in **Figure 5**. The waxed paper and holes acted as a filter for the larger salt granules, which is similar to the gas diffusion method used for uranium.

FIGURE 1

waxed paper

bowl

Cover bowl with waxed paper and secure with tape.

tape

FIGURE 2

needle

Poke 30 holes in waxed paper with needle.

FIGURE 3

salt   flour

spoon

Pour flour, then salt on surface of waxed paper.

FIGURE 4

spoon

Rub salt and flour mixure on surface of waxed paper.

FIGURE 5

waxed paper

salt

flour

bowl

When the waxed paper is raised, the bowl will be filled with mostly flour and very little salt.

Centrifuge Enrichment Simulation

A centrifuge is a cylindrical device that spins. When substances are placed in it, centrifugal force causes the heavier materials to separate and move toward the outer surface.

You can make a sneaky centrifuge to demonstrate this technique.

What's Needed

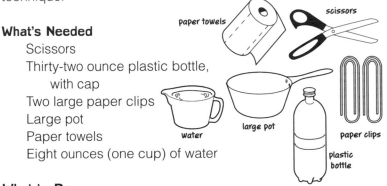

Scissors
Thirty-two ounce plastic bottle,
    with cap
Two large paper clips
Large pot
Paper towels
Eight ounces (one cup) of water

What to Do

First, carefully cut off the top third of the small bottle and use the points of the scissors to puncture small holes all around its body, as shown in **Figure 1**.

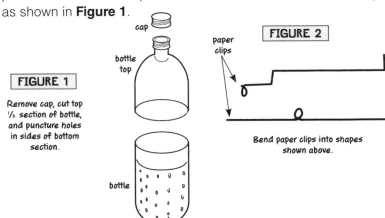

FIGURE 1

Remove cap, cut top
⅓ section of bottle,
and puncture holes
in sides of bottom
section.

FIGURE 2

Bend paper clips into shapes
shown above.

Bend the two paper clips into the shapes shown in **Figure 2**.

Next, connect the first paper clip with the center loop into the top holes on the side of the bottle. Then, attach the second paper clip into the first one's center loop hole. See **Figure 3**. They will act as a handle and stirring lever for the bottle.

Place the bottle cap into the bottom of the pot and then place the bottle on top of it. Place paper towels inside the bottle and pour 8 ounces of water onto the paper towels. See **Figure 4**.

Now turn the paper clip handle rapidly to spin the bottle. Keep the bottle spinning for about five minutes. Afterward, examine the paper towels to see how much they've dried and check the pot for water droplets. See **Figure 5**.

You'll discover that the centrifugal force removed water from the towels through the holes in the bottle and into the pot.

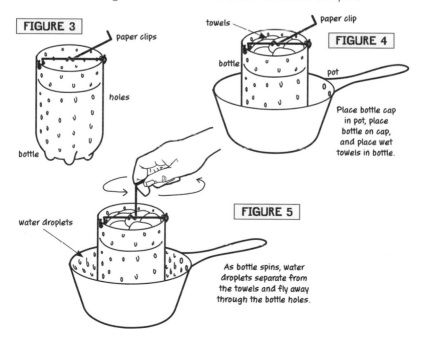

FIGURE 3

paper clips

holes

bottle

towels — paper clip

FIGURE 4

bottle

pot

Place bottle cap
in pot, place
bottle on cap,
and place wet
towels in bottle.

water droplets

FIGURE 5

As bottle spins, water
droplets separate from
the towels and fly away
through the bottle holes.

Nuclear Energy Simulation

This project will illustrate the multiple stages of nuclear energy production and power distribution, using everyday items. It's a perfect simulation for a school science project. First, let's review how nuclear energy is produced and converted into a form that can be used by consumers.

Similar to other power plants, nuclear power plants produce heat energy to boil water into steam that runs a turbine, which in turn powers an electrical generator. The main difference is that the heat is generated from a nuclear reaction (fission) in a lead-lined reactor, rather than without fission from burning coal.

Radioactive material, such as uranium, is mined and enriched, as discussed in Nuclear Fission Simulation. Once the U-235 materials are collected, they are stored as pellets inside aluminum rods. When placed near other rods, stray neutrons will start a nuclear fusion chain reaction, producing tremendous heat energy. To control the nuclear fission process, control rods are placed near them.

Control rods have pellets of cadmium or boron inside them, which absorb neutrons to halt the fission reaction. The control rods are placed between the U-235 rods in a matrix pattern (U-235 rod, control rod, U-235 rod, and so on), as shown in **Figure 1**.

When the control rods are lifted up and away from the U-235 rods, the fission reaction accelerates and heat is given off. The heat is used to turn water into steam, which turns an electrical turbine generator.

This project will show the four stages of a nuclear reactor in action, using household items.

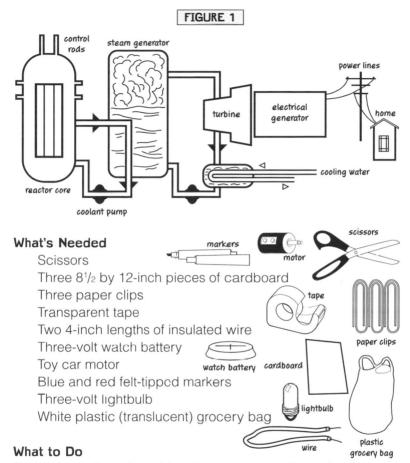

| FIGURE 1 |

control rods
steam generator
power lines
turbine
electrical generator
home
cooling water
reactor core
coolant pump

What's Needed

markers
motor
scissors
tape
paper clips

Scissors
Three 8½ by 12-inch pieces of cardboard
Three paper clips
Transparent tape
Two 4-inch lengths of insulated wire
Three-volt watch battery
Toy car motor
Blue and red felt-tipped markers
Three-volt lightbulb
White plastic (translucent) grocery bag

watch battery   cardboard
lightbulb
wire   plastic grocery bag

What to Do

Cut a piece of cardboard into the shape and dimensions shown in **Figure 2**. Be sure to cut the slits in the corners.

Bend two paper clips into an **S** shape and tape them to the center of the board. See **Figure 3**.

Strip the insulation from the ends of the two wires and tape one on each side of the watch battery, as shown in **Figure 4**.

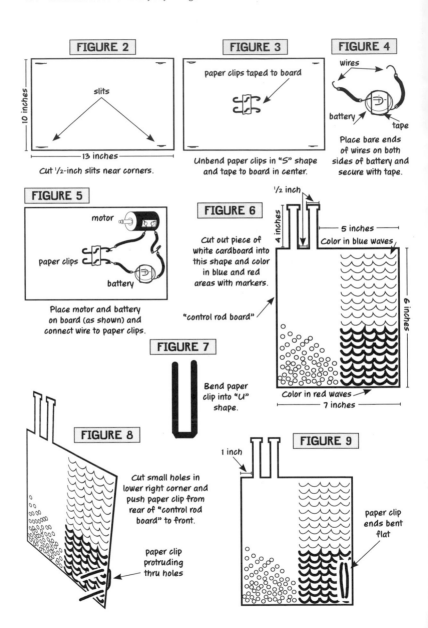

FIGURE 2

10 inches

slits

13 inches

Cut ½-inch slits near corners.

FIGURE 3

paper clips taped to board

Unbend paper clips in "S" shape and tape to board in center.

FIGURE 4

wires

battery

tape

Place bare ends of wires on both sides of battery and secure with tape.

FIGURE 5

motor

paper clips

battery

Place motor and battery on board (as shown) and connect wire to paper clips.

FIGURE 6

½ inch

4 inches

5 inches

Color in blue waves

6 inches

Cut out piece of white cardboard into this shape and color in blue and red areas with markers.

"control rod board"

Color in red waves

7 inches

FIGURE 7

Bend paper clip into "U" shape.

FIGURE 8

Cut small holes in lower right corner and push paper clip from rear of "control rod board" to front.

paper clip protruding thru holes

FIGURE 9

1 inch

paper clip ends bent flat

Next, position the battery and motor on the cardboard. Connect the wires in series from the paper clips to the motor to the battery, as shown in **Figure 5**.

Cut out the second piece of cardboard in the shape and dimensions shown in **Figure 6**. Notice the control rod "handles" at the top. Draw the neutron chain reaction onto the cardboard to represent the U-235 atom fission process of electrons bombarding other atoms, splitting them, and continuing the chain reaction: on the right side of the cardboard, draw blue water waves on the top half and red water waves on the bottom. The red shows the steamy, hot water from the heating process.

Next, bend a paper clip into a **U** shape. See **Figure 7**. Cut small holes in the control rod board's right corner area (the same corner as your red water waves). Push the paper clip through the holes from the back and bend the ends flat. See **Figures 8** and **9**.

When the control rod board is positioned properly on the main board, the "red water wave" paper clip will contact the other two paper clips and complete the electrical circuit, activating the motor. See **Figure 10**.

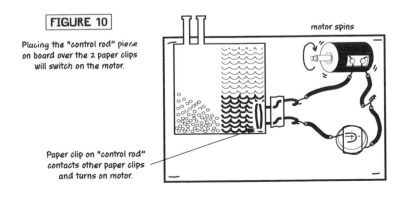

| FIGURE 10 |

Placing the "control rod" piece on board over the 2 paper clips will switch on the motor.

motor spins

Paper clip on "control rod" contacts other paper clips and turns on motor.

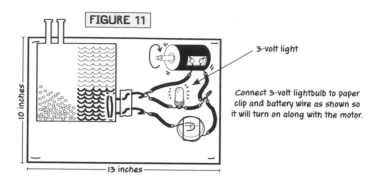

FIGURE 11

10 inches

13 inches

3-volt light

Connect 3-volt lightbulb to paper clip and battery wire as shown so it will turn on along with the motor.

Next, connect the light's wires across the motor's wires so it will turn on with the motor. See **Figure 11**.

Cut two strips of spare cardboard and tape them to the sides of the control rod board, to ensure that it slides in a straight path. See **Figure 12**.

Next, cut a piece of cardboard into the dimensions and shape shown in **Figure 13**. Notice the tabs on each corner. They will later fit into the main board's corner slots. Also cut out sections for the reactor core, steam generator, electrical generator (motor), and house window. Turn the cover board over, and cut out and tape white translucent plastic over the cutout sections.

Last, insert the cover board's tabs into the main board's slots and test to see if all three boards fit properly. Test the movement of the control rod board to ensure that it will activate the motor and light. See **Figure 14**.

When all of the sections fit and work properly, sliding the control rod up will show the reactor core's nuclear fission chain reaction, which generates steam and turns the turbine. This activates the electrical generator and distributes power to light the house. See **Figure 15**.

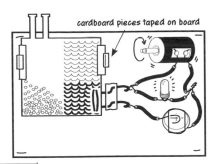

FIGURE 12

Cut 2 pieces of cardboard and tape them to the main board to act as guide rails so the "control rod" board slides straight.

cardboard pieces taped on board

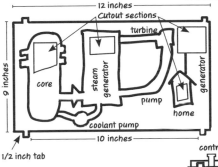

12 inches

Cutout sections

turbine

9 inches

core

steam generator

pump

generator

home

coolant pump

10 inches

1/2 inch tab

FIGURE 13

Cut a piece of cardboard into the size and shape shown. Notice cutout sections for the motor and 3-volt lightbulb to be seen through.

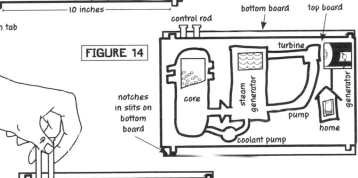

bottom board

top board

control rod

turbine

notches in slits on bottom board

core

steam generator

pump

generator

home

coolant pump

FIGURE 14

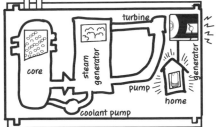

turbine

core

steam generator

pump

generator

home

coolant pump

PART IV
Bonus Sections

**Sneaky Uses for Everyday Things and
Sneakier Uses for Everyday Things Project Updates**

If you weren't aware by now, this book is the third in the *Sneaky Uses* series. As time goes on, you discover better ways of doing things. That's what this bonus section is about. It provides updates to projects and techniques found in *Sneaky Uses for Everyday Things* and *Sneakier Uses for Everyday Things*.

Sneaky project updates from *Sneaky Uses for Everyday Things* include little-known sources for superstrong magnets found in everyday things, an improved magnetically sensitive switch, a direction-finding update, and a Sneaky Magnifier.

Updates to projects found in *Sneakier Uses for Everyday Things* include a simple-to-make static electricity tester, more Hide and Sneak techniques for passwords and personal identification numbers, and several Gadget Jacket updates and options.

Sneaky Direction Finding

In the *Sneaky Uses for Everyday Things* project Road Scholar: Down-to-Earth Direction Finding, readers learned that even without a compass, there are numerous ways to find directions in desolate areas. Here's another sneaky one:

What's Needed

Stick or branch about 3 feet long
Rock or leaf

What to Do

On a sunny day, you can find out which direction is north, south, east, or west by using shadows. Stand a stick upright in the ground, as shown in **Figure 1**. Notice the shadow it casts and, using a rock or leaf, mark the shadow's edge.

Wait about fifteen minutes and notice the new shadow that appears. Mark its tip, too. See **Figure 2**. Draw an imaginary line between the two marks. This is the east–west line (west is the first tip, and the second marker represents east). You can draw an imaginary or real line across the east–west line to determine the north and south directions. See **Figure 3**.

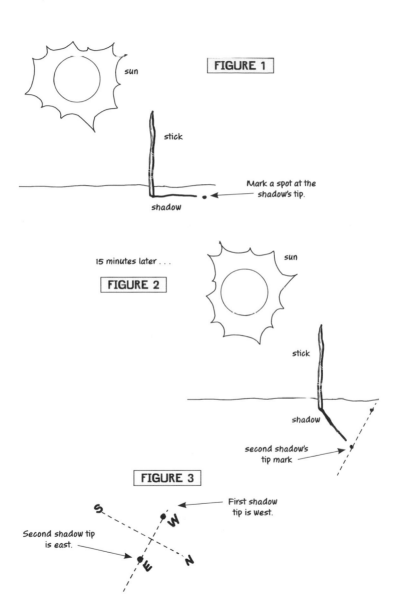

FIGURE 1

sun

stick

shadow

Mark a spot at the shadow's tip.

15 minutes later . . .

FIGURE 2

sun

stick

shadow

second shadow's tip mark

FIGURE 3

First shadow tip is west.

Second shadow tip is east.

S

W

N

E

Sneaky Magnifier

In the *Sneaky Uses for Everyday Things* project Make a Sneaky Magnifier, readers learned techniques to see tiny objects by using household objects. Here's a bonus Sneaky Magnifier you can make with paper:

What's Needed
    Needle or paper clip
    Paper or cardboard

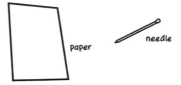

What to Do
If you're having trouble focusing on a small object or fine point, this Sneaky Magnifier will come in handy. Simply use a needle or paper clip to poke a small hole in a piece of paper (preferably a dark color), as shown in **Figure 1**.

Place the paper over the object, and you will see that the image is now enlarged. See **Figure 2**.

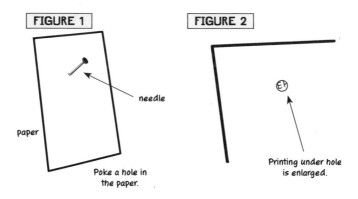

Poke a hole in the paper.

Printing under hole is enlarged.

Sneaky Magnet Sources

In *Sneaky Uses for Everyday Things* project Make a Power Ring, readers learned how to attach a magnet to a ring, to control devices. Here's are additional sneaky sources for superstrong, miniature magnets:

Superstrong magnets can be found in the most unlikely everyday items. For instance, miniature radio-controlled (RC) toy cars, the type that can fit in the palm of your hand, use a very strong, tiny magnet for steering. If you obtain a broken, discarded RC car, pry the body off its frame and remove the tiny magnet located between the front wheels. See **Figure 1**.

Some hearing-aid battery packages include a tiny, strong magnet to prevent the batteries from falling when the device is removed from its packaging. You can easily extract the magnet and use it for your own projects. See **Figure 2**.

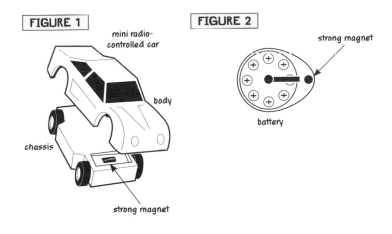

FIGURE 1

mini radio-controlled car

body

chassis

strong magnet

FIGURE 2

strong magnet

battery

Some toy dart kits use a metal board and powerful magnets on the tip of each of the darts. See **Figure 3**.

If you have a broken shaker-style flashlight, the type that uses no batteries, you can unscrew its case to access its superstrong magnet, as shown in **Figure 4**.

Sneaky Use for Magnets

You can test monetary currency for validity by folding a bill in half, as shown in **Figure 5**, and aiming the magnet near its edge. Real currency, unlike a counterfeit, has iron particles in the ink and will move toward a strong magnet.

Strong magnets can activate such devices as bulbs and buzzers, as shown in the next Sneaky Switch project.

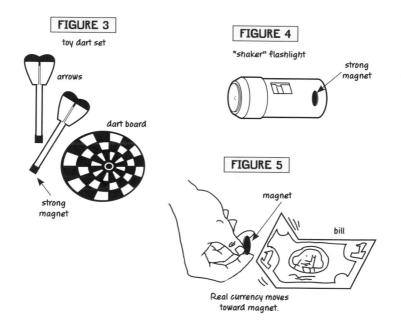

FIGURE 3
toy dart set
arrows
dart board
strong magnet

FIGURE 4
"shaker" flashlight
strong magnet

FIGURE 5
magnet
bill
Real currency moves toward magnet.

Sneaky Switch

In the *Sneaky Uses for Everyday Things* project Make Power Ring-Activated Gadgets, readers learned how to produce a switch that turns on when a magnet is in close proximity. Here's another way to design it for improved visual clarity (for science projects), using everyday things:

What's Needed

AA-size battery
Small 1¹/₂-volt lightbulb
Transparent tape
Cardboard
Paper clip
Stiff copper wire
Strong magnet

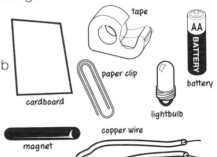

tape

cardboard

paper clip

magnet

AA BATTERY

battery

lightbulb

copper wire

What to Do

In this project, the parts are mounted with tape to a piece of cardboard (a postcard will work fine) so the operation of the Sneaky Switch can be seen by others or recorded on a digital camera.

First, place the battery and bulb end to end and tape them to the cardboard, as shown in **Figure 1**.

Next, bend the paper clip in the shape shown in **Figure 2**, so it wraps around the battery's positive (+) terminal.

Then, wrap the stiff copper wire around the bulb's base and bend it so it hovers over the paper clip, as shown in **Figure 3**. Place a piece of tape on the end of the paper clip to secure it to the board.

Last, ensure that the paper clip is bent upward slightly and is very close but not touching the copper wire above it. It should be able to move freely. Bring the strong magnet close to the top of the copper wire. The paper clip should move upward toward the magnet, contacting the copper wire and lighting the bulb as shown in **Figure 4**.

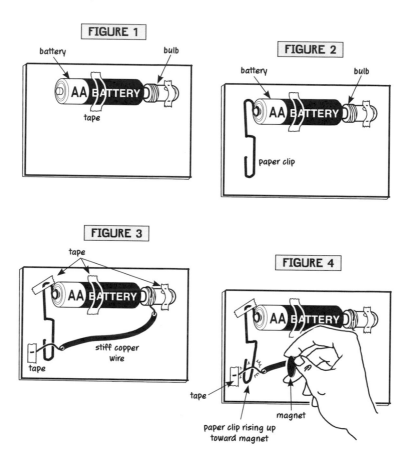

Gadget Jacket

Sneaky Sleeve Pocket

In *Sneakier Uses for Everyday Things,* readers learned how to make Sneaky Pockets, including a quick-release sleeve pocket, using fabric, elastic, and Velcro material. This updated project illustrates a simpler way to make a quick-release Sneaky Sleeve Pocket to access such devices as a pen, camera, flashlight, or calculator.

What's Needed

- Scissors
- Cloth
- Needle
- Thread
- Double-stick Velcro strips
- Jacket

What to Do

First, cut the cloth in the dimensions shown in **Figure 1**. Fold the material in half and use the needle and thread to sew it along the top and left side. See **Figure 2**.

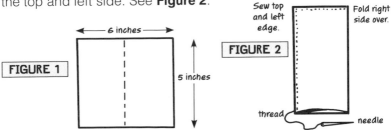

Apply two Velcro strips to the inside area of the lower sleeve of the jacket as shown in **Figure 3**. Next, turn the pocket inside out so the edges are smooth. Cut one side of the pocket so two small strips of fabric form latches, and apply small Velcro strips to them. Also apply Velcro strips on the back of the pocket. See **Figure 4**. **Figure 5** shows how the pocket appears when the latches are closed.

Place the pocket in the sleeve and press firmly so the Velcro secures it, as shown in **Figure 6**. When the pocket is attached inside the sleeve by the Velcro strips latched together, you can use your little finger to pry open the pocket latch. Your desired device will slide into the palm of your hand. See **Figure 7**.

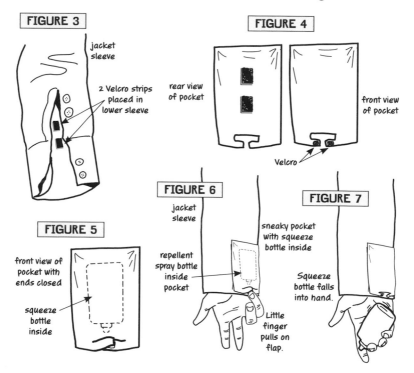

FIGURE 3

jacket sleeve

2 Velcro strips placed in lower sleeve

FIGURE 4

rear view of pocket

front view of pocket

Velcro

FIGURE 5

front view of pocket with ends closed

squeeze bottle inside

FIGURE 6

jacket sleeve

repellent spray bottle inside pocket

Little finger pulls on flap.

FIGURE 7

sneaky pocket with squeeze bottle inside

Squeeze bottle falls into hand.

Camera and Memory Drive

In *Sneakier Uses for Everyday Things,* Sneaky Collar, readers learned how to add devices to their gadget jacket's collar (with quick-release Velcro strips). Here are two additional applications:

What's Needed

Scissors
Double-stick Velcro strips
Mini digital camera
Jacket
USB flashdrive

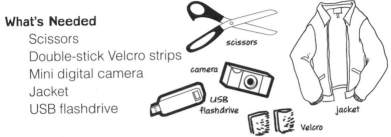

What to Do

Miniature digital, keychain cameras are now commonplace, can fit in the palm of your hand, and are available for under ten dollars. Many of them even have a video-recording mode. Adding one to the Gadget Jacket allows you to be ready to capture once-in-a-lifetime events.

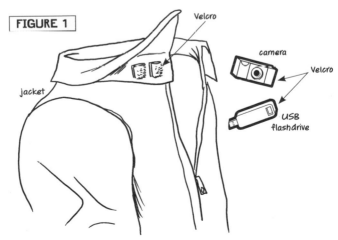

To mount the camera to the jacket, cut out small square pieces of Velcro. Apply them to the back of the camera and the matching Velcro pieces inside the collar area of the jacket. See **Figure 1**.

With many USB flashdrives now priced under five dollars, it makes sense to always have one with you. You can store text, graphics, music files, videos, and even entire Web sites on these miniature storage devices. Adding a flashdrive to your jacket will allow you to obtain and share files with others without having to log on to the Web. Plus, you'll have a convenient way to copy files from other computers whenever they are needed. With Velcro strips, the flashdrive always will be at hand.

Simply apply the appropriate Velcro strips to the flashdrive and under the collar area of the jacket, as shown in **Figure 2**, and you're ready to go.

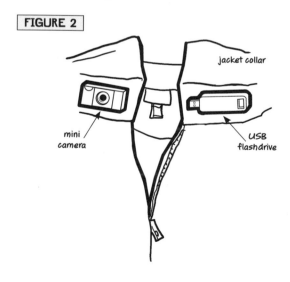

FIGURE 2

jacket collar

mini camera

USB flashdrive

Sneaky Static Electricity Tester

In *Sneakier Uses for Everyday Things,* readers learned how to construct an Electroscope, a Static Electricity Tester. Here's a simpler one you can make:

What's Needed

Large paper clip
Plastic cup or jar
Scissors
Aluminum foil
Comb or balloon

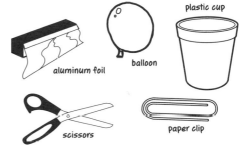

aluminum foil

balloon

plastic cup

scissors

paper clip

What to Do

To make a supersimple static electricity tester, bend the paper clip into the **S** shape shown in **Figure 1**. Place the paper clip on the edge of the cup. See **Figure 2**.

Next, cut two strips of aluminum foil, 1/2 inch by 2 inches, and bend one end so they can be placed on the paper clips, as shown in **Figure 3**.

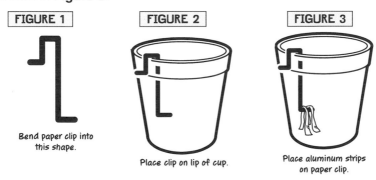

| FIGURE 1 | FIGURE 2 | FIGURE 3 |

Bend paper clip into
this shape.

Place clip on lip of cup.

Place aluminum strips
on paper clip.

Last, rub a comb or balloon on your hair or sweater and touch it to the top of the paper clip. You'll see the foil strips move. See **Figure 4**.

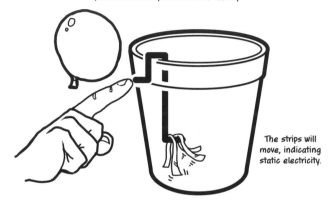

FIGURE 4

Rub a balloon against clothing and touch the paper clip.
Or, walk across carpet and touch the clip.

The strips will move, indicating static electricity.

Hide and Sneak: Password and Personal Information Protection

You probably have a written record of your computer passwords and personal information numbers (PINs) that you need to keep hidden. Hiding your information is not hard but, to be on the safe side, you should assume that it could be found.

This project illustrates three sneaky methods of encoding your personal information so that in case it's found, it still can't be used by others.

Crease Message Encryption

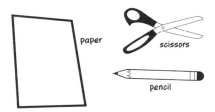

What's Needed
Piece of paper
Pencil
Scissors

paper

scissors

pencil

What to Do
Fold a piece of paper in half and then fold it down to a square as shown in **Figure 1**. Next, unfold the paper, as shown in **Figure 2**, so you can see the center crease.

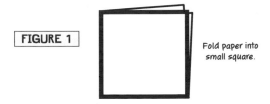

FIGURE 1

Fold paper into small square.

Then, write your password or message along the crease. See the example shown in **Figure 3**.

Last, write words on the paper that seem to describe an event or a message to disguise the secret cipher. See **Figure 4**. If the message is found, it will seem to be a simple message but you can follow the crease to discern the secret message.

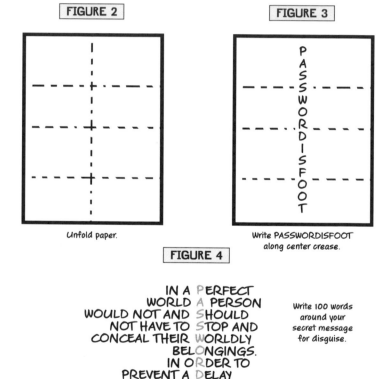

FIGURE 2

Unfold paper.

FIGURE 3

Write PASSWORDISFOOT along center crease.

FIGURE 4

IN A PERFECT
WORLD A PERSON
WOULD NOT AND SHOULD
NOT HAVE TO STOP AND
CONCEAL THEIR WORLDLY
BELONGINGS.
IN ORDER TO
PREVENT A DELAY
IN RETRIEVING
THEM. BE SURE TO
PLAY FAIR
WITH OTHERS
AND YOU SHOULD
APPEAR ATTRACTIVE.

Write 100 words
around your
secret message
for disguise.

Scroll Message Encryption

What's Needed
Scissors
Piece of paper
C-size battery
Pencil

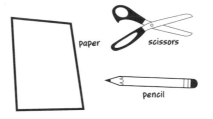

paper

scissors

pencil

battery

What to Do
Cut a ½ by 11-inch strip of paper as shown in **Figure 1**. Tightly wrap the strip around a C-size battery and write your message across the strip from left to right. See **Figure 2**.

When you unwrap the strip, your original message is not intelligible. You can write more letters on the scroll to further disguise the message.

To recover your secret message, simply wrap your scroll around a C-size battery or similarly sized cylinder.

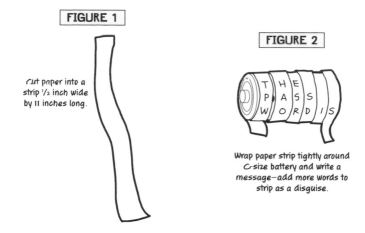

FIGURE 1

Cut paper into a strip ½ inch wide by 11 inches long.

FIGURE 2

Wrap paper strip tightly around C-size battery and write a message—add more words to strip as a disguise.

Label Code Encryption

To hide a record of one of your PIN codes, you can write a number code that refers to letters on a popular product label. If someone finds the code, it will not seem to have any meaning.

What's Needed
Product label
Pencil

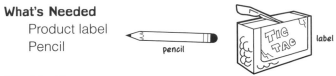

pencil

label

What to Do
Be sure to select an easy-to-obtain, popular product that can be found in locations other than your home (in case you need to retrieve your PIN while traveling).

In the example shown in **Figure 1**, a mint package label is used for the code. On a piece of paper, write two letters to represent the product—TT for Tic Tac, in this example.

The numbers that follow represent the letters on a phrase you select from the product label, in order of appearance. The code TT 3, 2, 10, 14, 16, 24 represent the message: Tic Tac SECRET.

You can produce similar codes using other product labels, including the larger label on the back of the product.

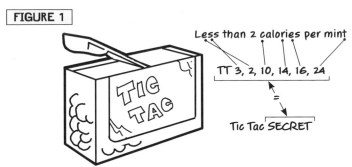

FIGURE 1

Less than 2 calories per mint

TT 3, 2, 10, 14, 16, 24

=

Tic Tac SECRET

Sneaky Uses for a Magnet

Magnets are one of the most versatile items for use with resourceful projects. They are used in telephones, computers, doorbells, electronic door locks, maglev (magnetic-levitation) trains, tape recorders, car crushers, scrap metal sorters, speakers, electric motors, generators, and more.

Here are more sneaky applications for magnets:

Parts Locater: An old antenna glued to a magnet makes a great parts locator. See **Figure 1**.

Tape Eraser: A magnet, when stroked near recording tape, will erase its contents. See **Figure 2**.

Cereal Iron Separator: Iron-fortified particles can be separated from cereal by placing magnets at the bottom of a bowl. See **Figure 3**.

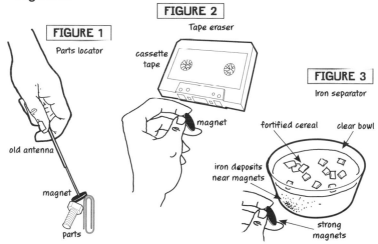

FIGURE 1
Parts locator
old antenna
magnet
parts

FIGURE 2
Tape eraser
cassette tape
magnet

FIGURE 3
Iron separator
fortified cereal
clear bowl
iron deposits near magnets
strong magnets

Levitator: Bend a large paper clip into a stand for a disk
magnet, and a smaller paper clip, connected by a thread,
will magically hover just below the magnet at the top. Turn
the stand sideways or upside down, and spin the little paper
clip for more fun. See **Figure 4**.

Magnet Maker: Stroke a thin piece of steel, iron, or tin at
least twenty times in the same direction and you'll make it
magnetic. See **Figure 5**.

Compass Maker: Stroke a needle at least twenty times in the
same direction and, when it hangs or floats, it'll point north
and south. See **Figures 6** and **7**.

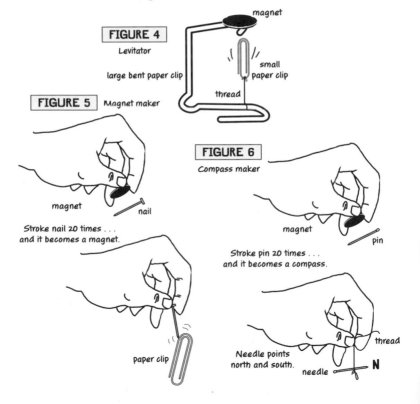

FIGURE 4

Levitator

magnet

large bent paper clip

small paper clip

thread

FIGURE 5 Magnet maker

FIGURE 6

Compass maker

magnet

nail

Stroke nail 20 times . . .
and it becomes a magnet.

magnet

pin

Stroke pin 20 times . . .
and it becomes a compass.

paper clip

Needle points
north and south.

thread

needle

N

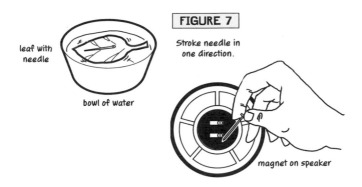

FIGURE 7

leaf with needle

bowl of water

Stroke needle in one direction.

magnet on speaker

You will find more sneaky magnet projects throughout this book. See the following projects for details:

Buzzer

Motor

Magnetic Switch

Electrical Generator

Tape Design Wiggler

Quiz Tester

Science and Technology Resources

If you find that you like science and want to go still further in your quest for knowledge, this section provides a multitude of science education resources. It contains links to city, state, and national science fairs; science camps and schools; science organizations; and educational scholarships.

You'll also find special inventor resources and contests, grants and awards, free government programs, educator lesson plans, and additional links to free science project Web sites.

Check out some of the resource sites listed to see what free projects and fantastic career opportunities await you.

Science Freebies, Grants, and Scholarships
Community of Science www.cos.com
Education Freebies www.thehomeschoolmom.com/
    teacherslounge/freebies.php
Science Magazine www.sciencemag.org
Science Master www.sciencemaster.com
Science Teacher Freebies www.teacherhelp.org/freebies.htm
Siemens Foundation www.siemens-foundation.org
U.S. Government Science Grants www.science.doe.gov/grants

Inventors and Inventing
About Inventors http://inventors.about.com/od/campinventio1/
    index_r.ht

AMA Science www.sciencetoymaker.org
American Solar Energy Society www.ases.org
Association of Science: Technology Centers www.astc.org
Biodiesel Board http://biodiesel.org
By Kids for Kids www.bkfk.com
The Discovery Channel: Young Scientist Challenge www.
    discovery.com/dcysc
Electric Auto Association http://eaaev.org
Energy Information Administration www.eia.doe.gov
Energy Star www.energystar.gov
Exploratorium www.exploratorium.edu
Funology www.funology.com
Intel Science Talent Search www.sciserv.org
Inventors Digest http://inventorsdigest.com
Inventors HQ www.inventorshq.com/just %20for %20kids.htm
Inventor Resources http://invention.lifetips.com/cat/61342/kid-
    inventors-internet-resources/index.html
National Ethanol Vehicle Coalition http://e85fuel.com/index.php
National Geographic Kids www.nationalgeographic.com/ngkids/
    index.html
Nuclear Energy Institute www.nei.org
Plug in America http://pluginamerica.com
Science Toymaker www.funology.com
Smart Homeowner www.smart-homeowner.com
United Inventors Association www.uiausa.com
Wind Works www.wind-works.org/index.html
Women in Technology www.witi.com/index-c.shtml
Yahooligans http://yahooligans.yahoo.com/Science_and_Nature/
    Machines/Inventions/Inventors

Science Fairs

Children's Museum List www.childrensmuseums.org/visit/reciprocal.htm

More Science Centers www.astc.org/sciencecenters/find_scicenter.htm

Science Centers Worldwide http://physics.usc.edu/ScienceFairs and www.cs.cmu.edu/~mwm/sci.html

Science Camps www.campresource.com

Science Camps for Girls www.sallyridecamps.com and www.sme.org

Science Catalogs www.amasci.com/suppliers.html

U.S. Government Science Resources http://sciencedems.house.gov/resources/science_education.htm

Energy-Saving Information

http://auto.howstuffworks.com/alternative-fuel-channel.htm

www.consumerenergycenter.org/errebate

www.ecohome.org

Energy Efficiency and Renewable Energy www.eere.energy.gov and www1.eere.energy.gov/consumer/tips/

www.energystar.gov/

www.epa.gov/epahome/athome.htm

www.findsolar.com

www.homepower.com

http://savepower.lbl.gov

http://science.howstuffworks.com/fuel-cell.htm

http://science.howstuffworks.com/nuclear-power.htm

www.solarcooking.org

www.windenergy.com

www.windturbine.net

Web Sites of Interest
Have fun devising and making your own sneaky jacket adaptations and be sure to check for additional ideas (and post your own) at www.sneakyuses.com.

Science Sites
amasci.com
build-it-yourself.com
discovercircuits.com
exploratorium.edu
howtoons.net
kidsinvent.org
sciencetoymaker.org
sneakyuses.com
theteachersguide.com/QuickScienceActivities.html
us.brainium.com
uspto.gov/go/kids
wildplanet.com

Frugal and Thrift Sites
choose2reuse.org
freegiftclub.net
frugalcorner.com
frugalitynetwork.com
getfrugal.com
make-stuff.com
ready-made.com
Recycle.net
thefrugalshopper.com
thriftydeluxe.com
wackyuses.com
watchthepennies.com

Gadgets Sites

advanced-intelligence.com
berberblades.com
casio.com
colibri.com
dailygadget.com
equalizers1.com
girltech.com
gizmodo.com
ijustgottahavethat.com
inventorsdigest.com
johnson smith.com
leatherman.com
netgadget.net
nutsandvolts.com
popgadget.net
robotstore.com
scientificsonline.com
smartplanet.net
spy-gear.net
spyderco.com
spymall.com
swissarmy.com
swisstechtools.com
the-gadgeteer.com/cgi-bin/redirect.cgi/gadget
thinkgeek.com
topeak.com
undercovergirl.com

Survival Sites

americansurvivalist.com
backwoodshome.com

backwoodsmanmag.com
basegear.com
beprepared.com
campmor.com
emergencypreparednessgear.com
equipped.com
fieldandstream.com
hikercentral.com/survival
homepower.com
productsforanywhere.com
ruhooked.com
secretsofsurvival.com
self-reliance.net
simply-survival.com
Survival.com
survival-center.com
Survivaliq.com
survivalplus.com
Survivalx.com
wildernesssurvival.com
wilderness-survival.net
windpower.org

Home Security Sites
mcgruff.org
ncpc.org
safesolutionsystems.com
X10.com
youdoitsecurity.com

Science and Technology Sites
about.com

boydhouse.com/crystalradio
craftsitedirectory.com
discover.com
hallscience.com
homeautomationmag.com
howstuffworks.com
johnson-smith.com
midnightscience.com
radioshack.com
scienceproject.com
scientificsonline.com
scitoys.com
thinkgeek.com
wildplanet.com

Other Web Sites of Interest

almanac.com
beprepared.com
casio.com
doityourself.com
equalizers1.com
movie-mistakes.com
nitpickers.com
popsci.com
popularmechanics.com
rube-goldberg.com
smarthome.com
tbotech.comrotorsportz.com
thefunplace.com
tipking.com
toollogic.com

Recommended Books

David Borgenicht and Joe Borgenicht, *The Action Hero's Handbook* (Quirk Books)

Robert Young Decton, *Come Back Alive* (Doubleday)

Dept. of the Air Force, *U.S. Air Force Search & Rescue Handbook* (The Lyons Press)

Dept. of the Army, *U.S. Army Survival Handbook* (The Lyons Press)

Simon Field, *Gonzo Gizmos* Simon (Chicago Review Press)

Ira Flatow, *They All Laughed . . . From Light Bulbs to Lasers: The Fascinating Stories Behind the Great Inventions That Have Changed Our Lives* (Perennial)

Joey Green, *Clean It! Fix It! Eat It!: Easy Ways to Solve Everyday Problems with Brand-Name Products You've Already Got Around the House* (Prentice Hall)

———. *Clean Your Clothes with Cheez Wiz: And Hundreds of Offbeat Uses for Dozens More Brand-Name Products* (Prentice Hall)

———. *Joey Green's Encyclopedia of Offbeat Uses for Brand-Name Products* (Prentice Hall)

Lois H. Gresh and Robert Weinberg, *The Science of Superheroes* (John Wiley & Sons)

William Gurstelle, *Backyard Ballistics* (Chicago Review Press)

Garth Hattingh, *The Outdoor Survival Handbook* (New Holland Publishers)

Vicky Lansky, *Another Use for 101 Common Household Items* (Book Peddlers)

———. *Baking Soda: Over 500 Fabulous, Fun, and Frugal Uses* (Book Peddlers)

———. *Don't Throw That Out: A Pennywise Parent's Guide* (Book Peddlers)

———. *Transparent Tape: Over 350 Super, Simple, and Surprising Uses* (Book Peddlers)

Hugh McManners, *The Complete Wilderness Training Book* (Dorling Kindersley)

Forrest M. Mims III, *Circuits and Projects* (Radio Shack)

———. *Science and Communications Circuits and Projects* (Radio Shack)

Steven W. Moje, *Paper Clip Science* (Sterling Publishing Co., Inc.)

Bob Newman, *Wilderness Wayfinding: How to Survive in the Wilderness as You Travel* (Paladin Press)

Tim Nyberg and Jim Berg, *The Duct Tape Book* (Workman Publishing Company, 1994)

———. *Duct Tape Book Too: Real Stories* (Workman Publishing Company)

———. *The Ultimate Duct Tape Book* (Workman Publishing Company)

Larry Dean Olsen, *Outdoor Survival Skills* (Chicago Review Press)

Joshua Piven and David Borgenicht, *The Worst-Case Scenario Survival* (Chronicle Books)

———. *The Worst-Case Scenario Travel* (Chronicle Books)

Royston M. Roberts, *Serendipity* (John Wiley & Sons)

Jim Wilkinson and Neil A. Downie, *Vacuum Bazookas, Electric Rainbow Jelly, and 27 Other Saturday Science Projects* (Princeton University Press)

John Wiseman, *The SAS Survival Handbook* (Harvill Books)

Magazines

Backpacker
Craft
E Magazine
Make
Mother Earth News
Nuts and Volts
Outdoor Life
Outside
Poptronics
Popular Mechanics
Popular Science
ReadyMade